UNDERSTANDING MAPLE

Maple is a powerful symbolic computation system that is widely used in universities around the world. This short introduction gives readers an insight into the rules that control how the system works, and how to understand, fix, and avoid common problems.

Topics covered include algebra, calculus, linear algebra, graphics, programming, and procedures. Each chapter contains numerous illustrative examples, using mathematics that does not extend beyond first-year undergraduate material. Maple worksheets containing these examples are available for download from the author's website. The book is suitable for new users, but where advanced topics are central to understanding Maple they are tackled head-on. Many concepts which are usually absent from introductory books and manuals are described in detail.

With this book, students, teachers, and researchers will gain a solid understanding of Maple and how to use it to solve complex mathematical problems in a simple and efficient way.

UNDERSTANDING MAPLE

IAN THOMPSON
University of Liverpool

CAMBRIDGE
UNIVERSITY PRESS

CAMBRIDGE
UNIVERSITY PRESS

University Printing House, Cambridge CB2 8BS, United Kingdom

One Liberty Plaza, 20th Floor, New York, NY 10006, USA

477 Williamstown Road, Port Melbourne, VIC 3207, Australia

314-321, 3rd Floor, Plot 3, Splendor Forum, Jasola District Centre, New Delhi - 110025, India

103 Penang Road, #05-06/07, Visioncrest Commercial, Singapore 238467

Cambridge University Press is part of the University of Cambridge.

It furthers the University's mission by disseminating knowledge in the pursuit of education, learning and research at the highest international levels of excellence.

www.cambridge.org
Information on this title: www.cambridge.org/9781316628140
10.1017/9781316809761

© Ian Thompson 2017

First published 2017

A catalogue record for this publication is available from the British Library

ISBN 978-1-316-62814-0 Paperback

Additional resources for this publication at www.cambridge.org/maple

Contents

Acknowledgements   *page* viii

1   Introduction   1
   1.1   Why This Book?   2
   1.2   The Maple Interface   3
   1.3   How to Read This Book   4

2   Getting Started   6
   2.1   Configuring the Interface   6
   2.2   The Help System   9
   2.3   Statements and Execution   10
   2.4   Spaces, Line Breaks and Comments   16
   2.5   Execution Groups   18
   2.6   Sections   19
   2.7   Displayed Results and Return Values   19
   2.8   Obtaining Approximate Results   21
   2.9   Elementary Functions   24
   2.10 Complex Numbers   27
   2.11 Variables   31
   2.12 Names   34
   2.13 Automatic Simplification and Evaluation   37
   2.14 Concatenation   42
   2.15 Relational Operators   44
   2.16 Sequences   48
   2.17 Sets and Lists   49
   2.18 Indices   53
   2.19 Element-wise Operations   56
   2.20 The seq, add and mul Commands   58
   2.21 Types   62

2.22   Packages   65

3   **Algebra and Calculus**   71
3.1   Manipulating Expressions   71
3.2   Extracting Parts of an Expression   76
3.3   Substitutions   79
3.4   Functions   81
3.5   Limits   87
3.6   Summing Series   89
3.7   Differentiation   92
3.8   Integration   94
3.9   Series Expansions   97
3.10   Assumptions   99

4   **Solving Equations**   103
4.1   Solving Single Equations   103
4.2   Solving Multiple Equations   107
4.3   Solving Approximately   109
4.4   Differential Equations   113

5   **Linear Algebra**   117
5.1   Creating Matrices and Vectors   117
5.2   Accessing Vector and Matrix Entries   120
5.3   Displaying Matrices and Vectors   122
5.4   Addition, Multiplication and Scalar Products   123
5.5   Vector Products and Norms   125
5.6   Other Matrix Operations   127
5.7   Solving Linear Systems   129
5.8   Copying Matrices and Vectors and Testing for Equality   129

6   **Graphics**   133
6.1   Creating Basic Plots   133
6.2   Customising a Plot   135
6.3   Parametric and Polar Plots   137
6.4   Three-Dimensional Plots   138
6.5   Combining Plots   140
6.6   Plots from Data   141

	6.7	Animations	144
7	**Programming**		**147**
	7.1	Conditional Statements	147
	7.2	Do Loops	150
	7.3	Nesting and printlevel	158
	7.4	The print and printf Commands	159
	7.5	Arrays	162
	7.6	Tables	168
8	**Procedures**		**174**
	8.1	A Basic Procedure	174
	8.2	The Structure of a Procedure	176
	8.3	Local and Global Variables	178
	8.4	Arguments and Parameters	183
	8.5	Checking Argument Validity	189
	8.6	Data Returned by Procedures	191
	8.7	Returning Unevaluated	192
	8.8	Output Displayed from Within Procedures	195
	8.9	Remember Tables and Recursion	195
	8.10	Viewing a Procedure Definition	197
9	**Example Programs**		**200**
	9.1	Pascal's Triangle	200
	9.2	The Collatz Problem	203
	9.3	A Newton–Raphson Iteration	205
	9.4	Sorting Data	208
	9.5	Quadrature Formulae	211
	9.6	Necklaces	215
Appendix A	**Other Ways to Run Maple**		219
Appendix B	**Terminating Characters**		223
	Index of Maple Notation		225

Acknowledgements

The author gratefully acknowledges the assistance of Dr Martyn Hughes, for his careful reading of several drafts, and also the reviewers appointed by Cambridge University Press and the development team at Maplesoft, for their many constructive suggestions. Thanks must also go to Maplesoft's technical support staff, for answering numerous questions of varying quality. However, the most substantial acknowledgement is due to the students and colleagues who have brought their difficulties with Maple to the author's attention. Many of the examples in this book were motivated by their problems.

1

Introduction

He would keep on trying to do this or that with a grim persistence that was painful to watch . . .

John Wyndham, 'The Day of the Triffids' [1]

Maple is a computer program capable of performing a wide variety of mathematical operations. It originated in the early 1980s as a computer algebra system, but today this description doesn't really do it justice. Maple has facilities for algebra, calculus, linear algebra, graphics (two- and three-dimensional plots, and animations), numerical calculations to arbitrary precision, and many other things besides. It is widely used in universities across the world, and is particularly useful for tasks that are tedious and error-prone when performed by humans, such as manipulating complicated series expansions and solving large sets of simultaneous equations. Used correctly, Maple can save time and quickly solve problems that would otherwise be intractable. Used incorrectly, it can lead to frustration, and the destruction of expensive IT equipment.

At the time of writing, the current version is Maple 2016. Versions before Maple 2015 were numbered starting from 1; the last of these was Maple 18. New features introduced in each version from Maple 4.0 onwards can be viewed using the help system (see Section 2.2). For the most part, recent changes have been relatively minor, at least as far as the material in this book is concerned. Consequently, all of the examples work with both Maple 2015 and Maple 2016. In fact, most will work in older versions as well, though naturally the number of exceptions increases the further back one goes. Two substantial new features are the `dataplot` command, discussed in Section 6.6, and the new rules concerning terminating characters, described in Appendix B (see also Section 2.3). Both of these were introduced in Maple 2015.

---

[1] Penguin Books, 1954. Reprinted by permission of Pollinger Limited (www.pollingerltd.com) on behalf of the Estate of John Wyndham.

1.1 Why This Book?

This book is intended for students, teachers and researchers who will ultimately wish to use Maple for advanced applications. Here, 'advanced' means something more complex than evaluating a single integral, but not necessarily designing and running a simulation of the latest jet engine. The book is suitable for undergraduates and postgraduates taking a course in which Maple is used, and for researchers who intend to use Maple for part of their work. It can also serve as a consolidation guide for users who already have some knowledge of Maple, but find themselves unable to decipher and eliminate certain error messages, or who currently rely on apparently magic recipes for solving problems, based on commands or operations whose meaning is not clear. There is no reliance on magic recipes here. Every feature we use is properly explained, with references to the online documentation where appropriate. The book is not a comprehensive reference guide (already available via the help system; see Section 2.2), nor is it a beginner's guide in the normal sense. It most certainly is not a 'guide for dummies'. We start from the beginning, assuming no prior knowledge of the subject whatsoever, but where advanced topics are central to understanding Maple they are tackled head-on, even as early as Chapter 2. In particular, the evaluation rules are a regular feature throughout. These determine the order in which input is processed by Maple. In most circumstances they are fairly simple (Section 8.4 discusses some more complex situations), but they are *absolutely crucial*.

Using this book, it is possible to tackle many complex problems without any additional Maple documentation. Readers can quickly progress to using packages and commands that have not been discussed, because the principles introduced apply across the whole system. Where the book alone is not sufficient, those who have read it will find themselves able to fully understand Maple's help pages, which can be rather technical, and the Maple Programming Guide (see Section 2.2), which is squarely aimed at very advanced users.

1.2 The Maple Interface

Users may interact with Maple in several different ways. One may proceed by typing commands, by using interface driven methods based on palettes and context menus, or by a combination of the two. The advantages and disadvantages of a particular method are not always obvious, though they may be hugely significant.

Interface driven methods can be very tempting to new users, because they may appear to eliminate the need to study a manual. For example, with the factory setting for input (2-D Math; see Section 2.1) it doesn't take much effort to work out how to sum series and evaluate integrals, using the Calculus and Expression palettes at the sides of the screen (if these are not visible, they can be revealed by choosing (Palettes) ▸ (Expand Docks) from the (View) menu). However, most users will eventually want to try something a little more complicated, in which case things are not quite so straightforward. For all its power, Maple is only a computer program, and as such it can only understand mathematical input that is structured in the correct way. Just as it is possible to type incorrect commands, it is also possible to use the palettes incorrectly, and construct something that a human mathematician might understand, but Maple does not. One way or another, technical issues will sometimes arise, and a solid understanding of Maple is needed to deal with these effectively. In view of this, interface driven methods don't save much time, unless the software is to be used exclusively for solving elementary problems. There will be no further discussion of such methods here (search for the User Manual in the help system for more information on the subject).

This book takes a command driven, or programmatic, approach to Maple, with the focus on the language rather than the interface. This has two principal advantages. First, it scales up very easily: the simple building blocks that make up the Maple language can be assembled to solve complex problems in an efficient way. This is where the real power of Maple lies. Second, there is transparency: a Maple worksheet constructed using a sequence of mouse clicks and menu selections is opaque in that a user opening it cannot see immediately (if at all) how it was created, or how it could be modified and adapted to his/her needs.

On the other hand, a worksheet composed from typed commands is 100% transparent. It may be that some users who master the Maple language later decide that more interface driven methods are suitable for some or all of their work. However, such users will continue to find this book valuable, because understanding the Maple language makes the behaviour of its interface far more tractable.

1.3 How to Read This Book

The technical material in this book is intended to be read in order and in its entirety. Great effort has been expended to keep the content short, while still covering all of the key points. Time has also been spent minimising the number of situations in which concepts are used before they are properly introduced. In a few places, these structural aberrations turn out to be unavoidable (or the lesser of two evils). Where this is the case, the simplest possible examples have been used to illustrate the issue at hand, and a reference to a later section, in which the out of place concept is dealt with in detail, is always given. At the very least, every reader should study Chapter 2. Most of this is very basic, but many fundamental aspects of Maple are described here, and without knowledge of these its behaviour can seem mysterious at best, and infuriating at worst. Chapters 3–6 depend heavily on Chapter 2, but less so upon each other. The majority of users will need the material in Chapters 3 and 4, which introduce Maple's symbolic computation facilities. Chapters 7–9 really need to be read in sequence. Without the ideas they contain, solving some problems will necessitate tedious, repetitive work, such as entering large numbers of very similar commands, which is not an efficient way to use Maple.

Throughout the book, items that appear in menus or dialogue boxes are shown in a rounded box with a grey background, such as (Help). Keystrokes such as [return] have a sharp-cornered box with a white background. Icons for toolbar buttons are shown as they appear in Maple 2016; the Maple 2015 version is also shown or described if it is significantly different. Small blocks of text marked with the symbol ★ are tips. These are useful (often very useful) but not vital pieces of information or advice. In some cases it is possible to deduce them from other parts of the book. Input and output is shown in the same style in which it appears in Maple itself (provided the configuration process explained in Section 2.1 is followed). In particular, Maple commands and statements are shown in a `typewriter typeface`. In a few places, Maple statements, or parts thereof, have been omitted in order to illustrate a larger or more general structure. Text in *italics* is used to give an indication as to what is missing. Output is omitted if showing it requires an inordinate amount of space. This convention is used extensively in Chapter 6, where plots drawn by Maple are not shown.

To get the most out of the examples throughout the book, it is necessary to execute them in Maple, and to experiment by modifying them. To save time for readers, the relevant files have been made available for download.[2] Typing the examples manually is fine, but it may be necessary to insert additional `restart` commands (see Section 2.11) between some of them to prevent unintended interactions, especially if the ordering is changed. The online worksheets already contain sufficient `restart` commands to ensure that everything works exactly as shown. Copying and pasting from an electronic version of the book may lead to unexpected results, and is therefore not recommended.

Please report errors to `ian.thompson@liverpool.ac.uk`.

---

[2] `pcwww.liv.ac.uk/~itho17/understanding_maple`

2

Getting Started

The quote is not worth two hundred dollars!

The author[1]

★ If Maple appears to freeze, try pressing the interrupt button (!) (the icon is a white hand inside a red stop sign in Maple 2015 and earlier) in the worksheet toolbar at the top of the window. You may need to wait a few seconds for this to take effect.

★ Due to the nature of Maple, it is not possible to entirely prevent it from crashing. This is very rare in modern versions, but you should still save your work frequently. In particular, the (Auto save) facility under (Tools) ▸ (Options) (Mac: (Maple 2016) ▸ (Preferences)) should always be enabled.

2.1 Configuring the Interface

The Maple *engine*, that is, the part of the software which processes data and performs calculations, can be accessed in several different ways. By far the most widely used is the Standard Worksheet Interface, which is started by clicking on the Maple icon, or by issuing the terminal command xmaple on some unix systems. It is probably fair to say that what most users refer to as 'Maple' is in fact the Standard Worksheet Interface (alongside the engine). However, there is also a Classic Worksheet Interface for 32-bit Windows machines, which places lower demands on system resources (in the past there was also a Classic Worksheet Interface for 32-bit Linux, but support for these platforms ended with Maple 2015). Finally, there is a command line version of Maple, which is useful for batch processing, and is briefly discussed in Appendix A. Elsewhere, it is

---

[1] Email to a representative of Pearson Education Inc.

assumed that the Standard Worksheet Interface is in use, though for the most part this affects only menus and toolbar buttons; nearly all Maple commands work in exactly the same way regardless of the interface.

Maple's Standard Worksheet Interface works with files called worksheets (with a lower case 'w'). Its two modes, Worksheet (with an upper case 'W') and Document, are used to create different types of worksheet. To add to the confusion, there are different ways to enter mathematical expressions, and these can be used in either mode. With the factory settings, mathematical input is generally expected in 2-D Math Notation. When an expression is typed in 2-D Math Notation, Maple reformats the input during entry, in an attempt to display mathematics as it would normally be written. For example, typing $\boxed{1}$ followed by $\boxed{/}$ causes a fraction to appear, and moves the cursor into the denominator. After entering the denominator, pressing the right arrow key moves the cursor outside the fraction (you can also use the mouse to reposition the cursor). Exponents behave in a similar way, so the sequence of keystrokes $\boxed{2}\ \boxed{\wedge}$ $\boxed{x}\ \boxed{\rightarrow}\ \boxed{/}\ \boxed{3}\ \boxed{\wedge}\ \boxed{y}\ \boxed{\rightarrow}\ \boxed{\rightarrow}$ produces the expression

$$\frac{2^x}{3^y}.$$

and moves the cursor outside the fraction, ready for entry of the next term. Unfortunately, the sequence of keystrokes used to construct a complex expression is not always evident from the display. When things go wrong (which they inevitably do in scientific computing — nobody gets everything right at the first attempt), getting out of trouble without deleting material and starting again can be very difficult, if it is possible at all. Therefore 2-D Math input is not recommended. Instead, the examples in this book are shown in Maple Notation (sometimes called 1-D Math Input), which is somewhat simpler. When expressions are entered using Maple Notation, Maple displays *exactly* what has been typed. The choice between Document Mode and Worksheet Mode is less important, but Maple sometimes reverts to 2-D Math input in Document Mode (regardless of its configuration), so Worksheet Mode is recommended. Both the $\boxed{\text{File}}$ menu and the Default home page offer users the options of opening a worksheet in either Document Mode or Worksheet Mode. However, some methods for creating new files will automatically cause a worksheet to appear in the default mode, which is Document under the factory settings. To avoid confusion, it is best to change this. The following steps can be used to make Maple Notation and Worksheet Mode the default options.

- ▸ On Linux or Windows, choose ⟨Options⟩ from the ⟨Tools⟩ menu.
  - ▸ On a Mac, go to the ⟨Maple 2016⟩ menu and select ⟨Preferences⟩.
- Select the ⟨Display⟩ tab.
- From the menu next to ⟨Input display⟩, choose ⟨Maple Notation⟩. Since there are no significant drawbacks to displaying *results* as they would be written by hand, changing ⟨Output display⟩ to something other than ⟨2-D Math Notation⟩ is not recommended.
- Now select the ⟨Interface⟩ tab.
- From the menu next to ⟨Default format for new worksheets⟩, select ⟨Worksheet⟩.
- You may also wish to turn off the Default home page, so that a blank worksheet appears instead when Maple is started. To do this, choose ⟨New, blank⟩ from the menu next to ⟨Open worksheet at startup⟩.
- Click ⟨Apply Globally⟩.

To check that this has worked, hold ⟨ctrl⟩ (Mac: ⟨cmd⟩) and press ⟨N⟩ to open a new worksheet in the default mode. Now type 'hello'. If the settings are correct this will appear in an upright (not italic) red or reddish brown typeface. The above process does not change the mode for any existing worksheets, so it may be worth quitting and restarting Maple at this point. Although the Maple language is largely independent of the input mode, there are some differences between the syntax rules for Maple Notation and the rules that apply to 2-D Math Notation. In addition, some menu items, buttons and shortcut keys may behave slightly differently in Document Mode. To be clear:

> Subsequent material in this book is written under the assumption that Worksheet Mode and Maple Notation are in use.

It is possible to *temporarily* change the input mode using the worksheet toolbar near the top of the window. Pressing (Text) will switch to Maple Notation, and pressing (Math) will activate 2-D Math Mode (alternatively, press [F5] to toggle between the two modes). The effect of this may not become apparent until some input is typed, though sharp-eyed users will notice a change in the appearance of the cursor. Adjustments to the input mode made in this way apply only in the vicinity of the current cursor location (strictly, they apply to commands entered under the current prompt; see Section 2.3 for more details). Elsewhere in the worksheet, the setting made under (Input display) remains in force.

★ To convert existing material from 2-D Math Notation (or any other form of input) into Maple Notation, highlight it, go to the (Format) menu and select (Convert To) ▸ (1D Math Input).

★ Colours and other font attributes can be changed via the style management dialogue, which is accessed by choosing (Styles) from the (Format) menu. Choose (Maple Input) or (2-D Output) from the list on the left of the dialogue box and then press (Modify) to change the format for input or output, respectively.

2.2 The Help System

Maple has a comprehensive help system, and it is important to learn to use this effectively. The help system can be accessed by choosing (Maple Help) from the (Help) menu at the top of the window, or by holding [ctrl] (on a Mac hold [cmd] instead) and pressing [F1]. The help system has a clickable table of contents and a search facility. The help pages themselves are connected by hyperlinks, allowing users to navigate between related topics easily. A particular help page can be loaded directly by entering a question mark followed by the command, operator or package with which assistance is needed. For example, entering `?plot` and pressing [return] displays the help page for the `plot` command. To access some help pages in this way, it is necessary to specify not just a topic, but also a subtopic, a subsubtopic and even a subsubsubtopic. For example, to find out about the new features of Maple 2016, one can enter `?updates,Maple2016,` whereas entering `?updates,Maple2016,AdvancedMath` leads directly to details of the new advanced mathematics features. Similar syntax can be used to show updates from as far back as Maple 8; for earlier versions execute `?updates,v` and use the list of results to the left of the help page (here v stands for version number, not version 5, which was called Maple V). Many of Maple's help pages contain a lot of technical details at the top, but there are examples at the bottom which can be cut and pasted into your worksheet.

★ Examples on a help page can be displayed in either 2-D Math Notation or Maple Notation. Press the button marked $\frac{x^2}{\llcorner x^2}$ in the context bar at the top of the help window to toggle between the two options.

Another useful resource is the Programming Guide, which can be accessed by executing `?ProgrammingGuide` or by searching for 'Programming Guide' from within the help system. The Programming Guide is intended for advanced users. It is very thorough, and contains a lot of information that is beyond the scope of this book.

2.3 Statements and Execution

When a new worksheet is opened (in Worksheet mode!), the cursor appears to the right of the *prompt symbol* >. Here, Maple expects a *statement*, a simple example of which is shown below.

```
> 2 + 2
```

Once a statement is complete, it can be executed by pressing return . Maple then displays the result, and the cursor moves down to a new prompt. A statement can be executed at any time by placing the cursor on it and pressing return , so if you make a mistake it's easy to go back and correct it; there is no need to type anything again. In Maple 18 and earlier, statements require a terminating character, which can be a colon or a semicolon. This requirement was relaxed in Maple 2015, but there are still some situations in which terminating characters are needed. To maintain backwards compatibility as far as possible, terminating characters will be included in all subsequent examples, even when they are optional. The rules that determine whether a terminating character is actually required are given in Appendix B (see also Section 2.7, where the effect of using a colon to terminate a statement is discussed).

Statements are usually typed, or copied and pasted from elsewhere in the worksheet, but you can also use the palettes on the sides of the window to help construct them. For example, clicking the π symbol under (Common Symbols) causes `Pi` to appear at the current cursor position. Some items in the palettes are not available when the input mode is set to Maple Notation (see Section 2.1). This is no great loss — the palettes can be useful for getting started, but later you are likely to find that they slow you down. Compare the time needed to construct the statement below using palettes with the time required to type it.

```
> cos( Pi / 2 ) ;
```
$$0$$

Note the cosine function in this example, which is referred to by its abbreviated name, as usual. Maple notation for most other elementary functions is equally self-explanatory, though some care is needed with logarithms; see Section 2.9 for more details.

★ Maple is case sensitive, so `pi` is not the same as `Pi`.

★ Check for typographical errors if Maple unexpectedly returns a statement (or part thereof) unevaluated.

```
> coz( 0 ) ;
```
$$coz(0)$$

★ Sometimes a suggested completion will pop up while you are typing. Press (return) to accept this, or continue typing to reject it.

★ To insert a prompt, move the cursor to the appropriate position, hold (ctrl) ((cmd) on a Mac) and press (K) or (J) to insert before or after the current cursor location, respectively. Alternatively, choose (Insert) ▸ (Execution group) ▸ (Before/After Cursor) with the mouse (execution groups are discussed in Section 2.5), or press the button marked ⟩_ in the worksheet toolbar to insert a prompt after the current cursor position (the icon was [> in Maple 2015 and earlier).

In general, Maple works with exact arithmetic unless explicitly told to do otherwise. This includes computations involving large integers and also fractions, surds, etc.

```
> 3^100 ;
```

$$515377520732011331036461129765621272702107522001$$

```
> 2 / ( 17 + 9 ) ;
```

$$\frac{1}{13}$$

```
> sqrt( 63 ) ;
```

$$3\sqrt{7}$$

In processing the last two statements, Maple simplifies $2/(17 + 9)$ and $\sqrt{63}$ to $1/13$ and $3\sqrt{7}$, respectively, but it does not automatically replace these with numerical approximations. The `evalf` command coerces Maple into computing a numerical approximation.

```
> evalf( Pi ) ;
```

$$3.141592654$$

```
> evalf( sqrt( 63 ) ) ;
```

$$7.937253933$$

Section 2.8 contains more details about approximations in Maple. Another important point to note is that parentheses () are used to group terms in a mathematical expression, and to enclose the argument(s) passed to a command. Square brackets and braces have different meanings in Maple and cannot be used in this way (see Sections 2.17 and 2.18). Consequently, an expression such as

$$\left[\frac{\{\sin(4) - 3\}^2 + 8}{4} - \cos\left(\frac{2}{7}\right)\right]^2$$

must be entered in Maple notation as follows.

```
> ( ( ( sin( 4 ) - 3 )^2 + 8 ) / 4 - cos( 2 / 7 ) )^2 ;
```

$$\left(\frac{1}{4}\left(\sin(4) - 3\right)^2 + 2 - \cos\left(\frac{2}{7}\right)\right)^2$$

★ When a closing delimiter is typed, a box flashes around the corresponding opening delimiter. Use this feature to help match parentheses
in complicated expressions.

★ Implied multiplication is not supported in Maple notation. Omitting
an asterisk will usually lead to an error message.

```
> 2 cos( Pi ) ;
Error, missing operator or `;`
```

However, in some circumstances Maple will accept the input and
produce a result which is almost certainly not what you want.

```
> 2( 3 - 1 ) ;
```

$$2$$

Here, $2(3 - 1)$ is interpreted as a function call, with the 2 referring to
the constant function whose value is 2 for every argument.

Maple applies arithmetic operations in the following order: ! comes
first, followed by ^, then / or *, and finally - or +. In other words, /
and * have the same level of precedence, as do - and +. The remaining
ambiguity is removed by the fact that statements are processed from left
to right unless the rules of precedence tell Maple to do otherwise. In
the next example, the result of the first statement is determined by the
fact that / takes precedence over +. The result of the second statement is
determined by the fact that Maple works from left to right.

```
> 6 / 2 + 1 ;
```

$$4$$

```
> 8 / 2 * 2 ;
```

$$8$$

Both of these statements could be disambiguated using the 'standard'
ordering of arithmetic operators used in mathematics (i.e. / followed by
*, + and finally -), but this fails twice in the next example, which shows
why Maple uses the left to right processing rule.

```
> 4 / 2 / 2 ;
```

$$1$$

```
> 5 - 1 - 1 ;
```

$$3$$

As usual, terms in parentheses are evaluated before the parentheses are removed; this can be used to change the order in which operations are applied.

```
> 4 / 2 * 3 ;
```

$$6$$

```
> 4 / ( 2 * 3 ) ;
```

$$\frac{2}{3}$$

```
> 3^3! ;
```

$$729$$

```
> ( 3^3 )! ;
```

$$1088886945041835216076800000$$

Maple provides several mechanisms that can be used to access the results produced by executing statements. Output can be copied and pasted, but the copy and paste operations must be repeated manually if earlier calculations are changed. Moreover, it is easy to forget that this is necessary when a saved worksheet is reopened some time after its creation. Therefore copying and pasting *output* should be avoided. Undoubtedly, the best method for storing and retrieving results is to use variables (see Section 2.11), but two other methods are useful in simple cases. First, the *ditto operator* % retrieves the last result that Maple computed.

```
> cos( Pi / 6 ) ;
```

$$\frac{1}{2}\sqrt{3}$$

```
> %^2 ;
```

$$\frac{3}{4}$$

It is also possible to use %% and %%% to access the penultimate result and the last but two, respectively. However, it is important to remember that the last three results are not necessarily the results of the three statements above the cursor position, and things can go horribly wrong when new statements are inserted into a worksheet that contains a lot of ditto operators.

★ All ditto operators start off empty when a new worksheet is started, or a saved worksheet is reloaded.

The second method for retrieving earlier results is provided by the equation labels. These are the black numbers in parentheses that appear on the right-hand side of the worksheet when Maple displays a result. To enter a reference to an equation label, hold ⌈ctrl⌉ (on a Mac hold ⌈cmd⌉ instead) and press ⌈L⌉, or choose (Label...) from the (Insert) menu, then type the number and press ⌈return⌉. The next example assumes that the statements are entered at the top of a new worksheet (otherwise the equation labels might be different).

> 1 / 10 + 1 / 100 ;

$$\frac{11}{100} \tag{1}$$

> (1)^2 ;

$$\frac{121}{10000} \tag{2}$$

In the second statement, the label (**1**) must be entered as described above; simply typing ⌈(⌉⌈1⌉⌈)⌉ won't work. The power ^2 is entered in the usual way. If new statements are inserted amongst existing statements, Maple will renumber the equation labels and update any references to them automatically. To avoid confusion caused by differing label numbers, this book does not show or use equation labels in any subsequent sections. Ditto operators will be used in very simple cases, and variables will be used elsewhere. Execute **?worksheet,expressions,equationlabels** for more about equation labels. Particular attention should be paid to the information concerning their behaviour upon restarting Maple.

By default, statements are not executed when a saved worksheet is reopened, even if the output they generated is still visible. However, in most cases everything can be restored by executing the whole worksheet: choose (Execute) ▶ (Worksheet) from the (Edit) menu, or press the button marked !!! in the toolbar to execute the entire worksheet. Worksheets that require their statements to be executed in an unusual order will cause problems, and should be avoided. There are also several mechanisms for storing statements in such a way that they will be executed automatically upon restarting. For more details, see `?worksheet,reference,initialization,?autoexecute` and `?worksheet,documenting,startupcode`.

2.4 Spaces, Line Breaks and Comments

In most situations, spaces in Maple notation are ignored.

```
> sin ( Pi / 4 ) ;
```

$$\frac{1}{2}\sqrt{2}$$

```
> sin(Pi/4);
```

$$\frac{1}{2}\sqrt{2}$$

However, names such as `sin` and `cos` and numbers with multiple digits must be treated as single entities, and cannot include spaces.

```
> co s( Pi ) ;
Error, missing operator or `;`
> 1 000 000 ;
Error, unexpected number
```

The same applies to operators, some of which are formed from more than one character. For example, `**` is an alternative notation for powers, so `4**2` is valid input, but Maple sees `4* *2` as two multiplications with the middle term missing, so it results in an error.

★ Spacing out Maple statements makes complex worksheets easier to read and debug. Errors such as erroneous minus signs can be difficult to spot if they are hidden in large blocks of unspaced code.

A line break, produced by holding `shift` and pressing `return` is usually treated in exactly the same way as a space (the end of a comment is an exception to this rule; see below). This feature can be used to keep long statements readable and to prevent them from running off the edge of the window. In the next example, a line break is inserted after the first line; pressing `return` alone at this point causes Maple to attempt execution, after which it complains about an incomplete statement.

```
> 1 + 2 + 3 + 4 + 5 + 6 + 7 + 8 + 9 + 10 + 11 + 12 + 13 +
   14 + 15 + 16 + 17 + 18 + 19 + 20 + 21 + 22 + 23 + 24 ;
```
$$300$$

Note that no new prompt appears when a line break is inserted.

★ Do not write excessively long lines (more than about 100 characters) of Maple code. Use `shift` and `return` to break them up.

After a *comment symbol* #, Maple ignores material until the end of the line. Use this facility to make your worksheet easier to understand, by inserting short explanations for statements whose effect is not obvious.

```
> # Obtain an approximation to e
> evalf( exp( 1 ) ) ;
```
$$2.718281828$$

Longer comments can be made using (∗ followed by ∗). Maple will ignore anything that appears between these, including line breaks.

```
> (*
   This will be ignored.
   So will this.
 *)
```

This feature is particularly useful for temporarily deactivating all or part of an execution group (see Section 2.5).

★ Empty lines can be used to space out worksheets and improve readability, but Maple doesn't always preserve these perfectly when saving and reloading. To ensure that a vertical space between two statements is maintained, use a line containing a single #.

Text that is more easily distinguishable from Maple statements can be inserted by choosing (Insert) ▸ (Paragraph) ▸ (Before/After Cursor) or pressing the button with the T icon in the worksheet toolbar. Formatting tools such as font choices, justification and colours are available from the toolbar near the top of the window. If necessary, insert an execution group (see Section 2.3) to return to the normal input mode.

2.5 Execution Groups

Immediately to the left of the prompt symbols (>), Maple displays black square brackets called *group ranges*. These show how the worksheet is divided into *execution groups*: two or more statements are members of the same group if and only if they are enclosed by the same bracket. Placing the cursor inside an execution group and pressing ⌈return⌉ once causes all of its statements to be executed in sequence. This makes execution groups ideal for situations in which one statement depends on the result of another. The simplest way to create an execution group is to place multiple statements on the same line, separated by colons or semicolons, but better readability is achieved by putting line breaks between the statements. Each execution group will usually receive a single equation label, which refers to the final result displayed when it is executed. The next example shows a simple execution group. Changing 736 to a different number and pressing ⌈return⌉ once will change both the exact and approximate results.

```
> sqrt( 736 ) ;
  evalf( % ) ;
```

$$4\sqrt{46}$$
$$27.12931993$$

Another indication of grouping is provided by the prompt symbols themselves. If there is no prompt between two statements then they are members of the same execution group. Throughout the remainder of this book, group ranges are omitted, and execution groups can be identified by the absence of prompts. However, it should be noted that it is possible for more than one prompt to appear in a group. For example, if a sequence of statements is copied and pasted from another application, each line will get its own prompt, but the statements will be placed in the same execution group. Additionally, prompt symbols are not deleted when existing groups are merged by highlighting and choosing ⬤Edit⬤ ▶ ⬤Split or Join⬤ ▶ ⬤Join Execution Groups⬤.

▼ **Worksheet Section Heading**

```
> evalf( Pi ) ;
  cos( % ) ;
```
$$3.141592654$$
$$-1.$$

```
> 2 + 2 ;
```
$$4$$

Figure 2.1 A worksheet section, containing two execution groups.

2.6 Sections

Worksheets can be divided into sections to aid organisation. To insert a section select (Insert) ▸ (Section), then type the heading, and move down to begin entering Maple statements. A section can be expanded or collapsed by clicking on the grey triangle to the left of the heading. Thus, a grey triangle pointing to the right ▸ is an indication that a section has been collapsed, and so some statements may be hidden. An expanded section is shown in Figure 2.1. A new section can be created from an execution group by placing the cursor on a statement inside the group and choosing (Format) ▸ (Indent). Similarly, to move an execution group outside a section, place the cursor on one of its statements and choose (Format) ▸ (Outdent). To move an execution group into an existing section, indent it, then highlight both sections and choose (Edit) ▸ (Split or Join) ▸ (Join Sections). Inside a section it is possible to create further divisions using subsections. Besides the fact that they cannot appear outside sections, subsections they work in much the same way and need not be discussed in any detail. Executing a worksheet (e.g. by pressing !!!) will expand and execute any collapsed sections and subsections.

2.7 Displayed Results and Return Values

To prevent Maple from displaying the result returned by a statement, terminate it with a colon. This feature is useful when performing calculations where you don't need to see the result of each intermediate step, especially in cases where these are very long. It is important to stress that using a colon does not prevent or delay any computations, it *only* affects the display. In particular, the result of a statement terminated by a colon is still available via a ditto operator (but not an equation label).

```
> 1000! :
> evalf( % / 2^8525 ) ;
```

$$21.08294067$$

★ Unwanted output produced by a statement can be permanently removed by changing the terminating semicolon to a colon and executing again (if you highlight and delete the output, it will reappear if the statement is executed again).

There are some statements which do not return results, though they may display some output. Statements of this type do not affect the values stored by ditto operators, and the output they display cannot be accessed using them (if an equation label is generated, this will still work in the usual way). In the next example, the ditto operator contains the value 12 after π is displayed, because the **print** command has no return value.

```
> 3 * 4 ;
```

$$12$$

```
> print( Pi ) ;
```

$$\pi$$

```
> % ;
```

$$12$$

See Section 7.4 for more about the **print** command. As a general rule, it is best to think of a return value as something that can be used in a later calculation, whereas output on the screen is just useful information for the user's benefit. For example, since the purpose of the **print** command is simply to display a message, adding it to a number doesn't make sense.

```
> 12 + print( Pi ) ;
```

$$\pi$$
$$12 + (\ )$$

On the other hand, the cosine function returns a number as its result, so it can be used in arithmetic expressions.

```
> 12 + cos( Pi ) ;
```

11

Where a statement does return a result, terminating with a semicolon does not necessarily mean that this will be displayed after execution. Roughly speaking, the result will not be displayed in full if this would generate an excessive amount of output, such as a huge matrix. This behaviour can be altered by changing the **rtablesize** interface variable (see Section 5.3). There are also situations in which one statement is placed inside another, and in these circumstances the rules governing which results are displayed are slightly more complicated. See Section 7.3 for more details. Again, none of this has any bearing on the computations that take place; only the display is affected.

2.8 Obtaining Approximate Results

A number that includes a decimal point is called a *floating point* value (or just *float* for short). When one of these is present in an arithmetic operation, it causes an effect called *contagion*, which means an approximate result will be produced, even if the other value involved is exact.

```
> 1.0 / 7 ;
```

0.1428571429

```
> 2^0.5 ;
```

1.414213562

In versions up to Maple 18, π was not affected by contagion, but this changed in Maple 2015.

```
> 4 * Pi / 3.0 ;
```

4.188790204   (Maple 2015 and later)

1.333333333 π (Maple 18 and earlier)

Unfortunately, this introduces an inconsistency: other mathematical constants are treated differently. For example, Euler's constant,

$$\gamma = \lim_{n \to \infty} \left(-\ln n + \sum_{j=1}^{n} \frac{1}{j} \right)$$

is known to Maple, but contagion cannot be used to reveal its approximate numerical value.

```
> 1.0 * gamma ;
```

$$1.0\,\gamma$$

```
> evalf( gamma ) ;
```

$$0.5772156649$$

Contagion from outside does not cause approximate function evaluations.

```
> 4.0 * sqrt( 3 ) ;
```

$$4.0\sqrt{3}$$

```
> sin( 3.0 ) / 7 ;
```

$$0.02016000116$$

When the first statement above is executed, the square root does not 'see' the factor 4.0; it only knows about its own argument. Since this is an exact value, Maple leaves $\sqrt{3}$ as it is. When the second statement is executed, the sine function receives a floating point argument, so an approximate evaluation is performed. Subsequently, the division operator receives one exact and one floating point argument, causing contagion, and an approximate final result. The most robust method for producing approximate results is the **evalf** command, which can be applied to all or part of an expression.

```
> evalf( sin( Pi / 12 ) ) ;
```

$$0.2588190451$$

```
> 2 * evalf( sin( 4 ) ) ;
```

$$-1.513604991$$

By default, Maple performs floating point arithmetic using ten significant decimal figures. An individual calculation can be performed using more digits (or fewer), as shown in the next example.

```
> evalf[ 100 ]( Pi ) ;
```

3.14159265358979323846264338327950288419716939937510582\
    0974944592307816406286208998628034825342117068

```
> evalf[ 4 ]( 2 * Pi ) ;
```

$$6.284$$

An older syntax with the same functionality is to provide the number of digits after the quantity to be evaluated, e.g. `evalf( Pi , 100 )`. This is still supported in Maple 2016, though it is no longer mentioned by the `evalf` help page. The precision level for the entire worksheet is controlled by the `Digits` environment variable. To change this, we need to use the *assignment operator* `:=`, which is discussed in detail in Section 2.11. A precision setting made in this way remains in force until Maple is restarted, or until a subsequent assignment is made to `Digits`.

```
> Digits := 100 ;
```

$$Digits := 100$$

```
> evalf( sqrt( 2 ) ) ;
```

1.41421356237309504880168872420969807856967187537694807\
    3176679737990732478462107038850387534327641573

```
> Digits := 10 ;
```

$$Digits := 10$$

```
> evalf( sqrt( 2 ) ) ;
```

$$1.414213562$$

★ The theoretical maximum number of digits may differ from one system to another, but on any modern computer it will be very large indeed. However, setting `Digits` anywhere near this value will render Maple so slow as to be unusable.

```
> kernelopts( maxdigits ) ;
```

$$38654705646$$

Note the `kernelopts` command, which is used to query (and in some cases set) variables that affect Maple's computation; execute `?kernelopts` for more details.

The number of digits used in performing a calculation is not necessarily the same as the number of correct significant figures in the result, which is often smaller.

```
> evalf[ 10 ]( Pi - 3.141 ) ;
```

$$0.000592654$$

Here, Maple evaluates π to ten significant figures, but four of these are cancelled by subtracting 3.141, so that only six digits are correct in the result. In general, there is no way to determine how many significant figures must be retained at intermediate steps in order to produce an answer with a given level of accuracy. There are also occasions when Maple returns results with greater precision than might be expected.

```
> fsolve( x^3 + 1 = 0 , complex ) ;
```

$$-1., 0.500000000000000 - 0.866025403784439\,\mathrm{I},$$
$$0.500000000000000 + 0.866025403784439\,\mathrm{I}$$

Here, the `fsolve` command (see Section 4.3 for more about this) approximates the roots of the cubic equation $x^3 + 1 = 0$, and the results are given to 15 significant figures. This happens because Maple opts to use the arithmetic facilities provided by the CPU, to increase performance. A detailed discussion of the differences between this hardware arithmetic and Maple's own software arithmetic is outside the scope of this book; execute `?HFloat` and `?evalhf` for more information. For our purposes, it is sufficient to note that (unless explicitly told to do so), Maple won't use hardware arithmetic if there is a risk that doing so could have a detrimental effect on accuracy.

2.9 Elementary Functions

Table 2.1 shows a list of Maple commands for elementary functions and their inverses. Trigonometric and hyperbolic functions are accessed by

Function	Command	Inverse
absolute value (modulus)	`abs( x )`	—
cosine	`cos( x )`	`arccos( x )`
sine	`sin( x )`	`arcsin( x )`
tangent	`tan( x )`	`arctan( x )`
hyperbolic cosine	`cosh( x )`	`arccosh( x )`
hyperbolic sine	`sinh( x )`	`arcsinh( x )`
hyperbolic tangent	`tanh( x )`	`arctanh( x )`
natural logarithm	`log( x )` or `ln( x )`	`exp( x )`
base 10 logarithm	`log10( x )`	`10^x` or `10**x`
base *b* logarithm	`log[ b ]( x )`	`b^x` or `b**x`
square root	`sqrt( x )`	`x^2` or `x**2`

Table 2.1 *Maple notation for elementary functions.*

typing their abbreviated names (i.e. `sin` for sine, etc.) and the prefix `arc` is used to obtain the inverse.

```
> cos( Pi / 4 ) ;
```
$$\frac{1}{2}\sqrt{2}$$

```
> evalf( sinh( 2 ) ) ;
```
$$3.626860408$$

```
> arcsinh( % ) ;
```
$$2.000000000$$

The real domains and ranges for the inverse trigonometric and hyperbolic functions are shown in Table 2.2, though it should be noted that elementary functions in Maple can also accept complex arguments and produce complex results; see Section 2.10. The inverse tangent function has the special property that it can accept either one or two arguments. With one real argument, it returns a result in the range $(-\pi/2, \pi/2)$. With two real arguments — a y coordinate followed by an x coordinate — it returns a result in the range $(-\pi, \pi]$. Generally, `arctan( y , x )` is preferable to `arctan( y / x )` because the two-argument form avoids the possibility of ending up in the wrong quadrant when $x < 0$, and also prevents division by zero in cases where $x = 0$.

Function	Domain	Range	Function	Domain	Range
arccos	$[-1, 1]$	$[0, \pi]$	arccosh	$[1, \infty)$	$[0, \infty)$
arcsin	$[-1, 1]$	$[-\pi/2, \pi/2]$	arcsinh	$\mathbb{R}$	$\mathbb{R}$
arctan	$\mathbb{R}$	$(-\pi/2, \pi/2)$	arctanh	$(-1, 1)$	$\mathbb{R}$

Table 2.2 *Real domains and corresponding ranges for inverse trigonometric and hyperbolic functions. In the case of* arctan, *the range is shown for the single argument form.*

```
> arctan( 1 / sqrt( 3 ) ) ;
```
$$\frac{1}{6}\pi$$

```
> arctan( 1 , sqrt( 3 ) ) ;
```
$$\frac{1}{6}\pi$$

```
> arctan( -1 , -1 ) ;
```
$$-\frac{3}{4}\pi$$

```
> arctan( 1 , 0 ) ;
```
$$\frac{1}{2}\pi$$

Both `ln( x )` and `log( x )` refer to the natural (base e) logarithm of x. The latter will also accept an index in square brackets, which can be used to change the base.

```
> log( 10.0 ) ;
```
$$2.302585093$$

```
> log[ 2 ]( 128 ) ;
```
$$7$$

The letter e does not represent the exponential function in Maple notation; the correct syntax for e^x is `exp( x )`. Indeed, sharp-eyed users will observe that e produces an italic *e* in the output, whereas `exp( 1 )` produces an upright version. As the next example shows, these are not the same entity.

```
> e ;
```

$$e$$

```
> log( % ) ;
```

$$\ln(e)$$

```
> exp( 1 ) ;
```

$$e$$

```
> log( % ) ;
```

$$1$$

There is a temptation to define e as a shorthand for exp(1) using the macro command, to save typing (an assignment to the variable e could also be used; see Section 2.11). As the following example shows, this has unfortunate side effects.

```
> macro( e = exp( 1 ) ) :   # Don't do this!
> evalf( e^20 ) ;
```

$$4.851651938 \ 10^8$$

```
> evalf( exp( 20 ) ) ;
```

$$4.851651954 \ 10^8$$

The last two digits in the first result are wrong, as can be shown by increasing precision and repeating the calculations (see Section 2.8). Raising e to the power x is often not the most accurate or efficient way to compute e^x, but this is exactly what storing and exponentiating exp(1) forces Maple to do.

★ In addition to elementary functions, Maple can work with standard special functions, as well as many more esoteric functions. To see the complete list, execute ?initialfunctions.

2.10 Complex Numbers

The imaginary unit is obtained using a capital I, and complex numbers are constructed by simply adding together their real and imaginary parts.

```
> I^2 ;
```
$$-1$$
```
> ( 3 + I ) * ( 1 - 2 * I ) ;
```
$$5 - 5\,I$$

Not surprisingly, the `conjugate` command computes complex conjugates.

```
> conjugate( 2 + I ) ;
```
$$2 - I$$

Maple allows complex numbers to appear in any mathematical operation where they make sense.

```
> sin( I * log( 2 ) ) ;
```
$$\frac{3}{4}\,I$$
```
> evalf( cosh( 1 + I ) ) ;
```
$$0.8337300251 + 0.9888977058\,I$$

The `Re` and `Im` commands are used to extract the real and imaginary parts of a complex number, and `abs` and `argument` can be used to compute the modulus and argument, with the argument taken to lie in the interval $(-\pi, \pi]$.

```
> Re( 2 + I ) ;
```
$$2$$
```
> Im( sin( 2 + I ) ) ;
```
$$\cos(2)\sinh(1)$$
```
> abs( 1 - I ) ;
```
$$\sqrt{2}$$
```
> argument( 1 - I ) ;
```
$$-\frac{1}{4}\,\pi$$

The `convert` command can be used to convert a complex number into polar form.

```
> convert( 1 + I , polar ) ;
```

$$\mathrm{polar}\left(\sqrt{2},\ \frac{1}{4}\pi\right)$$

The `polar` command can be used to construct complex numbers from their modulus and argument, but `evalc` (evaluate to complex) is needed to obtain a Cartesian result.

```
> polar( 1 , Pi / 2 ) ;
```

$$\mathrm{polar}\left(1,\ \frac{1}{2}\pi\right)$$

```
> evalc( % ) ;
```

$$\mathrm{I}$$

The `evalc` command can also be used to evaluate square roots and other fractional powers where the result is a complex quantity. This happens automatically in some cases, but not all.

```
> sqrt( 3 + 4 * I ) ;
```

$$2+\mathrm{I}$$

```
> sqrt( 1 + I ) ;
```

$$\sqrt{1+\mathrm{I}}$$

```
> evalc( % ) ;
```

$$\frac{1}{2}\sqrt{2+2\sqrt{2}}+\frac{1}{2}\mathrm{I}\sqrt{-2+2\sqrt{2}}$$

```
> (-1)^(1/2) ;
```

$$\mathrm{I}$$

```
> (-1)^(1/3) ;
```

$$(-1)^{1/3}$$

```
> evalc( % ) ;
```

$$\frac{1}{2}+\frac{1}{2}\mathrm{I}\sqrt{3}$$

Note that Maple uses the principal branch for fractional powers, so

$$z^{1/n} = \sqrt[n]{|z|}\,e^{i\arg(z)/n},\quad n\in\mathbb{N}.$$

★ Where such a result exists, a real root of a real number can be obtained
   using the **surd** command. To compute $\sqrt[n]{x}$ (which has the same sign
   as x), use **surd(x , n)**.

   > surd(-8 , 3) ;

$$-2$$

To avoid the need for **evalc** in obtaining a Cartesian result from input in
polar form, use exponentials.

> exp(I * Pi) ;

$$-1$$

> 4 * exp(I * Pi / 3) ;

$$2 + 2\,I\sqrt{3}$$

When Maple does not simplify a complex exponential it may be useful to
convert it into trigonometric form. This can be achieved using the **trig**
option for the **convert** command. There is also an **exp** option which
performs the reverse process.

> convert(exp(2 * I) , trig) ;

$$\cos(2) + I\sin(2)$$

> convert(cos(2) , exp) ;

$$\frac{1}{2}\,e^{2I} + \frac{1}{2}\,e^{-2I}$$

Maple allows users to change the notation it uses for the imaginary
unit. Most mathematicians prefer a lower case i, and many engineers
use j. The **interface** command can be used for this purpose.

> interface(imaginaryunit = i) ;

$$I$$

> i^2 ;

$$-1$$

This change remains in force until Maple is restarted, and leaves the
symbol I free to be used for another purpose. To avoid any confusion, the
default Maple notation will be used in subsequent examples involving
complex numbers. A final note concerns the result of the **interface**

command. When `interface` is used to change a variable, the old value (*1* in the above example) is returned. Displaying this is rarely useful, so it is usual to terminate statements of this type with a colon.

2.11 Variables

Variables are used to store data, and to retrieve the results of previous calculations. The *assignment operator* `:=` is used to assign a value to a variable.

```
> a := 27 ;
```
$$a := 27$$

```
> b := 4 ;
```
$$b := 4$$

```
> c := a + b ;
```
$$c := 31$$

Assignments are *not* equations. The expression to the right of the assignment operator is computed, and associated with the *name* on the left (names are discussed in more detail in Section 2.12). This means assignments can reference the variable that is being assigned.

```
> k := 3 ;
```
$$k := 3$$

```
> k := k + 1 ;
```
$$k := 4$$

On its own, the symbol `=` represents a relational operator (see Section 2.15 for more about these) which asserts that two quantities are equal. It cannot be used to make assignments.

```
> s = 3 ;
```
$$s = 3$$

```
> s ;
```
$$s$$

```
> u := 1 ;
```

$$u := 1$$

```
> u = u + 1 ;
```

$$1 = 2$$

★ If a Maple statement produces an unexpected (or nonsensical) result, check that all assignments have been made using : =, and not =, which doesn't work.

To delete the value of a variable, use the **unassign** command.

```
> a := 27 ;
```

$$a := 27$$

```
> unassign( 'a' ) ;
> a ;
```

$$a$$

Note the single right quotes around **a** in the argument to **unassign**. These prevent Maple from substituting 27 for a before attempting the unassignment, which would lead to an error. See Section 2.13 for more details, and also a useful shortcut for unassignment. The **restart** command is used to clear all variables and other definitions in Maple's memory, including values stored in ditto operators. It negates the effect of *almost* all statements. Execute **?restart** for a list of exceptions.

```
> m := 27 ;
```

$$m := 27$$

```
> n := 10 ;
```

$$n := 10$$

```
> restart ;
> m ;
```

$$m$$

```
> n ;
```

$$n$$

The **Describe** command can be used to make an enquiry about the current status of a variable. Generally this reveals more information than simply evaluating its name.

```
> k := 27 ;
```

$$k := 27$$

```
> k ;
```

$$27$$

```
> Describe( k ) ;

k::integer = 27
```

★ It is a good idea to include a **restart** command before starting work on a new problem. This includes the beginning of the worksheet; re-executing without a **restart** at the top may have unfortunate effects.

★ Values assigned to variables are not stored when a worksheet is saved. To restore them, it is necessary to execute the statements in which the assignments were made, for example by pressing the execute worksheet button (!!!). See Section 2.3 for more details.

Maple allows multiple assignments to be made in a single statement. This feature provides a neat shortcut for swapping the values of two variables. In the next example, the values of j and p are first swapped using a temporary, or scratch, variable called t, which is subsequently discarded. This is the standard technique in many programming languages. The change is then reversed in a single statement.

```
> j := 22 ;
```

$$j := 22$$

```
> p := 49 ;
```

$$p := 49$$

```
> t := j ;  # Swap by 'standard' method
```

$$t := 22$$

```
> j := p ;
```

$$j := 49$$

```
> p := t ;
```
$$p := 22$$
```
> unassign( 't' ) :
> j , p := p , j :   # Reverse swap using neat shortcut
> j ;
```
$$22$$
```
> p ;
```
$$49$$

Variables can be used to store strings (sequences of characters) and algebraic expressions as well as numbers. Strings are formed using *string quotes* ".

```
> s := "abc" ;
```
$$s := \text{"abc"}$$
```
> t := "def" ;
```
$$t := \text{"def"}$$
```
> p := x^2 + 4 * x + 4 ;
```
$$x^2 + 4x + 4$$
```
> q := x^2 - 7 * x - 1 ;
```
$$x^2 - 7x - 1$$
```
> p + q ;
```
$$2x^2 - 3x + 3$$

See Chapter 3 for more about algebra in Maple.

2.12 Names

Up to this point, simple names such as *a*, *b* and *c* have been used for variables. Longer names are possible as well.

```
> weasels := 5 :
> stoats  := 7 :
> weasels + stoats ;
```
$$12$$

Single left quotes ` are called *name quotes* in Maple. These can be used to create names that begin with a number, or that contain spaces.

```
> `Number of the beast` := 666 ;
```

$$Number\ of\ the\ beast := 666$$

Name quotes can be used to create names containing any character, and even names that consist solely of numbers. However, the result of this is likely to be rather confusing.

```
> `12` := 13 ;
```

$$12 := 13$$

```
> `13` := -13 ;
```

$$13 := -13$$

```
> `12` + `13` ;
```

$$0$$

Some names are replaced by corresponding symbols when they appear in the output from a Maple statement. These include Greek letters and the Hebrew letter aleph.

```
> aleph := 1 ;
```

$$\aleph := 1$$

```
> alpha := Gamma ;
```

$$\alpha := \Gamma$$

The last statement illustrates a general rule. If the first letter in the name of a Greek letter is capitalised, the corresponding upper case Greek letter is produced in the output. The letter π is an exception. In this case there are three forms: the lower case letter π, the number π and the upper case letter Π. The last of these is obtained using PI.

```
> evalf( pi ) ;
```

$$\pi$$

```
> evalf( Pi ) ;
```

$$3.141592654$$

```
> evalf( PI ) ;
```

$$\Pi$$

Most of Maple's own names are protected, so that trying to make assignments to them results in an error.

```
> Pi := 3.0 ;
Error, attempting to assign to `Pi` which is protected.
Try declaring `local Pi`; see ?protect for details.
```

Forcing the issue is unlikely to lead to good results, but it is possible.

```
> unprotect( Pi ) ;
> Pi := 3.0 ;
```

$$\pi := 3.0$$

```
> sin( Pi ) ;
```

$$0.1411200081$$

The same mechanism can be used to protect important user-defined variables. As with the **unassign** command discussed in Section 2.11, single right quotes are needed to prevent Maple from replacing the variable with its value before applying the protection.

```
> bank_balance := 1000000 :
> protect( 'bank_balance' ) :
> bank_balance := 0 ;
Error, attempting to assign to `bank_balance` which is
protected.  Try declaring `local bank_balance`; see
?protect for details.
```

★ To display all names that have been assigned a value (omitting those that are assigned by Maple itself), use the **anames** command with the **user** option.

```
> c := 1 :
> d := 2 :
> anames( user ) ;
```

$$d, c$$

2.13 Automatic Simplification and Evaluation

Maple usually performs two steps when it processes an expression: *automatic simplification* and then *evaluation*. Roughly speaking, automatic simplification performs simple operations, whereas complicated calculations must wait until the evaluation stage. There is no way to prevent automatic simplification, but evaluation of an expression can be prevented by enclosing it in single right quotes '. These are called *unevaluation quotes* in Maple.

```
> '1 + 1' ;
```

$$2$$

```
> x := 1 ;
```

$$x := 1$$

```
> '1 + x' ;
```

$$1 + x$$

```
> % ;
```

$$2$$

When the first of the above statements is processed, $1 + 1$ is automatically simplified to 2, so that the unevaluation quotes have no effect (note that they are removed by evaluation). However, variables are not replaced by their values during automatic simplification, so $1 + x$ is returned unevaluated in the result of the second statement. Only when the last statement is executed is $1 + x$ itself evaluated. In contrast, ditto operators are resolved by automatic simplification.

```
> x := 3 :
> 27 ;
```

$$27$$

```
> 'x + % + 4' ;
```

$$x + 31$$

```
> %
```

$$34$$

Apart from performing basic arithmetic operations, automatic simplification also reduces fractions to their lowest terms, removes unnecessary parentheses, computes integer powers and approximates fractional powers of floating point values.

```
> '( 1 + 1 ) / 4' ;
```

$$\frac{1}{2}$$

```
> '4^2' ;
```

$$16$$

```
> '9.0^(1/2)' ;
```

$$3.000000000$$

We have already encountered two applications for unevaluation quotes: deleting an assigned value for a variable in Section 2.11, and protecting user-assigned values in Section 2.12. There is a clever shortcut for unassignment.

```
> a := 27 ;
```

$$a := 27$$

```
> a := 'a' :   # Same effect as unassign( 'a' ) :
> a ;
```

$$a$$

This requires some explanation. The effect of evaluating `'a'` is just to remove the unevaluation quotes, so, after executing `a := 'a'`, the name *a* evaluates to itself.

Understanding when evaluation will occur and what its consequences are is the key to avoiding many of the most common pitfalls with Maple. In particular, in *most* situations, arguments undergo evaluation before being passed to commands. We will refer to this as prior evaluation. In the next example, $\pi/2$ is substituted for *x* before the sine function is invoked, which seems entirely sensible.

```
> x := Pi / 2 :
> sin( x ) ;
```

$$1$$

However, there are situations where this behaviour is not desirable.

```
> x := 2 :
> limit( sin( x ) / x , x = 0 ) ;
Error, invalid input: limit expects its 2nd argument, p,
to be of type Or(name = algebraic, set(name =
algebraic)), but received 2 = 0
```

Here, the `limit` command is apparently used to evaluate

$$\lim_{x \to 0} \frac{\sin x}{x}$$

(see Section 3.5 for more about `limit`), but this is derailed by the fact that the name x has been assigned the value 2 earlier in the worksheet. Consequently, after the arguments have been evaluated, what's left is a request to evaluate $\sin(2)/2$ as $2 \to 0$, which is nonsense. A well-placed `restart` command can be used to avoid this, but it will delete the values of all assigned variables. Alternatively, x can be unassigned individually (see Section 2.11), or a different symbol can be used. To work with the symbol x, regardless of whether it has already been assigned a value, use unevaluation quotes.

```
> x := 2 :
> limit( 'sin( x ) / x' , 'x' = 0 ) ;
```
$$1$$

Now the prior evaluation simply strips off the unevaluation quotes, so that the `limit` command receives a request to take the limit $x \to 0$ in the expression $\sin(x)/x$. It is important to keep in mind that x still has the value 2 at the end of the calculation, and will be evaluated if it appears again. Consider the following example.

```
> x := 0 :
> s := expand( ( 1 + 'x' )^2 ) ;
```
$$s := x^2 + 2x + 1$$

```
> s ;
```
$$1$$

Here, the `expand` command (see Section 3.1) is used to multiply out a bracket. Unevaluation quotes are used to prevent Maple from substituting 0

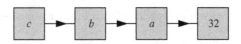

Figure 2.2 An assignment chain.

for x before carrying out the expansion. However, the result involves x, so s evaluates to 1 when the final statement is executed.

★ When a command produces an error, or an unexpected result, consider the effect that prior evaluation has on the argument(s), and use unevaluation quotes to prevent this where appropriate.

There are several types of evaluation in Maple, of which the most common is *full recursive evaluation*. This follows chains of assignments until their end. Consider the following example.

```
> c := b ;
```
$$c := b$$

```
> b := a ;
```
$$b := a$$

```
> a := 32 ;
```
$$a := 32$$

```
> c ;
```
$$32$$

Executing the first three statements creates an assignment chain, which is illustrated graphically in Figure 2.2. When the last statement is executed, c evaluates to b, then b evaluates to a and finally a evaluates to 32. This is the end of the assignment chain.

The **eval** command can be used to perform *n-level evaluation*. The next example again uses the assignment chain in Figure 2.2, and illustrates the result of applying one-, two- and three-level evaluation to c.

```
> c := b :
> b := a :
> a := 32 :
> eval( c , 1 ) ;
```

$$b$$

```
> eval( c , 2 ) ;
```

$$a$$

```
> eval( c , 3 ) ;
```

$$32$$

It is also important to understand how evaluation is influenced by unevaluation quotes. A full recursive evaluation removes one pair of quotes, and then stops. On the other hand, an n-level evaluation removes one pair of quotes at each step, but it stops if all pairs have been removed, even if n exceeds the number of quote pairs.

```
> ''sin( Pi )'' ;  # The first ...
```

$$'\sin(\pi)'$$

```
> % ;  # The second ...
```

$$\sin(\pi)$$

```
> % ;  # The third ...
```

$$0$$

```
> eval( ''sin( Pi )'' , 1 ) ;
```

$$'\sin(\pi)'$$

```
> eval( ''sin( Pi )'' , 3 ) ;
```

$$\sin(\pi)$$

Note that the double quotes in the above example are produced by pressing $\boxed{\,'\,}$ twice; they are not string quotes. Only the `eval` command without a second argument is strong enough to remove a set of quotes and perform the final evaluation.

```
> eval( 'sin( Pi )' ) ;
```

$$0$$

If it encounters multiple sets of unevaluation quotes, the `eval` command with no second argument removes two pairs, after which evaluation stops.

Two other forms of evaluation are worthy of brief mentions here, the first of which is *evaluation to a name*. In this process, Maple ceases evaluation when it reaches a valid name. By far the most prevalent case of evaluation to a name occurs on the left-hand side of assignments, where it is applied automatically. In many situations, the object on the left-hand side of an assignment is already a name, and nothing happens. However, there are cases (particularly those involving names with indices; see Section 2.18) in which this process is crucially important. Evaluation to a name can be applied to any object using the `evaln` command, though this is rarely needed.

```
> x := 35 ;
```

$$x := 35$$

```
> evaln( x ) ;
```

$$x$$

Finally, there is *last name evaluation*. There is no command to invoke this process; rather it is a property that certain objects possess. Formally, if an object is subject to last name evaluation rules, then any name assigned to that object will evaluate to itself. The effect of this is to create a barrier which stops evaluation one step earlier than might otherwise be expected. It is not possible to compose an instructive example of this based on material introduced so far, so we must content ourselves with a hypothetical example on the basis of Figure 2.2. If the number 32 were subject to last name evaluation rules, a full recursive evaluation of b, c or a would result in a (the last name in the chain). The barrier created by last name evaluation can be broken using `eval`. In our hypothetical example, applying `eval` to a, b or c (without a second argument) would return the result 32.

2.14 Concatenation

Objects such as names and strings can be joined together (concatenated) using the `cat` command. The simplest case involves concatenation of two strings.

```
> s := "abc" ;
```

$$s := \text{"abc"}$$

```
> t := cat( s , "def" ) ;
```

$$t := \text{"abcdef"}$$

The `cat` command can also append numbers to strings.

```
> cat( "The approximate value of pi is " , evalf( Pi ) ) ;
```

"The approximate value of pi is 3.141592654"

The empty string can be used to convert a number into a string.

```
> cat( "" , 123 ) ;
```

"123"

Note that the result of concatenating two numbers is a symbol (a type of name), not a number.

```
> s := cat( 1 , 2 ) ;
```

$$s := 12$$

```
> Describe( s ) ;

s::symbol = `12`
```

```
> s + 1 ;
```

$$12 + 1$$

The *concatenation operator* || provides an alternative syntax for concatenating objects. It has the rather unusual property that its left operand undergoes evaluation to a name, but not a full evaluation. In the next example, `cat( a , b )` forms the name *5b*, because *a* is evaluated to 5 before concatenation. On the other hand, a || b produces *ab*, because *a* is a valid name, so evaluation to a name has no effect.

```
> a := 5 ;
```

$$a := 5$$

```
> cat( a , b ) ;
```

5b

```
> a || b ;
```

ab

Another difference between || and `cat` is that a name created by ||
undergoes an immediate evaluation, whereas this does not happen to
names formed using `cat`.

```
> cd := 55 ;
```
$$cd := 55$$

```
> c || d ;
```
$$55$$

```
> cat( c , d ) ;
```
$$cd$$

```
> % ;   # Extra evaluation
```
$$55$$

Creating names by concatenating letters and numbers was common
practice in early versions of Maple. In the next example, `r || j` evaluates
to the name $r5$, and this variable is then assigned the value 36.

```
> j := 5 :
> r || j := 36 ;
```
$$r5 := 36$$

```
> r5 ;
```
$$36$$

Updates introduced in Maple 4.0 rendered this technique largely obsolete.
In modern versions, indexed data structures such as arrays and tables are
more flexible and easier to use (see Sections 7.5 and 7.6, respectively).
Use of the concatenation operator itself is also now discouraged; its own
help page (?||) recommends that the `cat` command should be used
instead, wherever possible.

2.15 Relational Operators

The *relational operators* shown in Table 2.3 are used to form equations
and inequalities. The left- and right-hand sides of such expressions can
be extracted using the commands `lhs` and `rhs`.

Name	Operator	Name	Operator
equal to	=	not equal to	<>
greater than	>	greater than or equal to	>=
less than	<	less than or equal to	<=

Table 2.3 *Maple notation for relational operators.*

```
> eqn := e = m * c^2 ;
```

$$eqn := e = mc^2$$

```
> lhs( eqn ) ;
```

$$e$$

```
> rhs( eqn ) ;
```

$$mc^2$$

When using **lhs** and **rhs** with inequalities, it is important to keep in mind that expressions involving > and ≥ are replaced by equivalent expressions using < and ≤ during automatic simplification. A good mnemonic here is that the left-hand side is always lower.

```
> a > b ;
```

$$b < a$$

```
> lhs( a > b ) ;
```

$$b$$

Methods for solving equations are discussed in Chapter 4. Here we introduce **evalb**, which tells Maple to evaluate an equation or inequality to a boolean value (i.e. *true* or *false*) if it can.

```
> evalb( 3 > 4 ) ;
```

$$false$$

```
> evalb( 0! = 1 ) ;
```

$$true$$

Any expression that can be evaluated to *true* or *false* is called a *conditional expression*, and can be used as the argument to **evalb**. This includes compound expressions formed using boolean operators such as **and**, **not** and **or**.

```
> a := 1 :
> b := 2 :
> c := 3 :
> evalb( b > a and b > c ) ;
```

$$false$$

```
> evalb( not a = b ) ;
```

$$true$$

```
> evalb( b > a or b > c ) ;
```

$$true$$

Some care is needed with constants such as π, and elementary function expressions that cannot be evaluated exactly. Tests for (in)equality will work, but otherwise exact symbolic quantities must be approximated before being used with **evalb**.

```
> evalb( Pi = sqrt( 2 ) ) ;
```

$$false$$

```
> evalb( 3 <> Pi ) ;
```

$$true$$

```
> evalb( sqrt( 2 ) > 0 ) ;
```

$$0 < \sqrt{2}$$

```
> evalb( evalf( sqrt( 2 ) ) > 0 ) ;
```

$$true$$

A potential pitfall with this occurs when values are close together. In this case, cancellation of leading digits can lead to incorrect results.

```
> evalb( evalf( 1 - exp( -25 ) ) < 1 ) ;
```

$$false$$

Here, $1 - \exp(-25)$ evaluates to 1, which is correct to ten significant figures, so the test wrongly returns *false*. Problems of this type can sometimes be avoided by a more careful construction of the statement or inequality. In the above example, applying **evalf** to the whole inequality allows automatic simplification to remove 1 from both sides before any approximation occurs. Subsequently, $-\exp(-25)$ evaluates to $-1.388794386 \times 10^{-11}$, which is clearly negative.

```
> evalb( evalf( 1 - exp( -25 ) < 1 ) ) ;
```

$$true$$

However, there are cases in which values are very close together and no simplification is possible. One way around this is to use increased precision (see Section 2.8), but the number of digits needed may not be obvious. The best approach is to use the **is** command, which guarantees the correct answer.

```
> p := sqrt( 2 ) * 2510613731736 / 1130173253125 ;
```

$$p := \frac{2510613731736}{1130173253125} \sqrt{2}$$

```
> evalf[ 20 ]( p - Pi ) ;
```

$$6.395 \ 10^{-16}$$

```
> evalb( evalf( p > Pi ) ) ;
```

$$false$$

```
> is( p > Pi ) ;
```

$$true$$

In fact, **is** can be used in place of **evalb** in most situations. However, **evalb** is more efficient in cases where both commands can be used. In addition, **is** returns *false* when names about which nothing is known are compared, which is potentially misleading, whereas **evalb** does nothing.

```
> is( f > 0 ) ;
```

$$false$$

```
> is( f <= 0 ) ;
```

$$false$$

```
> evalb( f > 0 ) ;
```

$$0 < f$$

```
> evalb( f <= 0 ) ;
```

$$f \le 0$$

In the above example, evaluation to a boolean would become possible later if f were to be assigned a numeric value. Both `evalb` and `is` return *FAIL* if they are applied to an expression that had no possibility of ever evaluating to a boolean.

```
> evalb( 1 + I > 1 - I ) ;
```

FAIL

```
> is( 1 + I > 1 - I ) ;
```

FAIL

2.16 Sequences

A collection of objects separated by commas is called a *sequence* in Maple. These often appear when a statement returns multiple results.

```
> solve( x^2 - 3 * x + 2 = 0 ) ;
```

$$2, 1$$

See Chapter 4 for more information about the `solve` command. No new Maple commands are needed to join sequences together, or to append new elements to the ends of an existing sequence. We need only consider the evaluation rules.

```
> s := a , b , c ;
```

$$s := a, b, c$$

```
> t := 1 , 2 , 3 ;
```

$$t := 1, 2, 3$$

```
> u := beta , s , t ;
```

$$u := \beta, a, b, c, 1, 2, 3$$

When the last statement is executed, s and t evaluate to a, b, c and $1, 2, 3$ before the assignment is made, so that the value associated with the name u is the sequence $\beta, a, b, c, 1, 2, 3$. Attempting to pass sequences as arguments to commands leads to a subtlety. A few commands, such as `max` and `min`, work in the obvious way, but many others will fail.

```
> r := 2 , 4 , 7 , 1 ;
```
$$2, 4, 7, 1$$

```
> max( r ) ;
```
$$7$$

```
> min( r ) ;
```
$$1$$

```
> member( 1 , r )
Error, invalid input: member expects 2 or 3 arguments, but
received 5
```

When the last three statements are processed, prior evaluation causes r to be replaced with $2, 4, 7, 1$ before the command is invoked. This doesn't cause a problem for `max` and `min`; these are very flexible and work with many structures, including sequences, and also sets and lists (Section 2.17), matrices and vectors (Chapter 5) and arrays (Section 7.5). However, the attempt to determine whether 1 is a member of the sequence r fails, because the `member` command actually receives the sequence of arguments $1, 2, 7, 4, 1$, which doesn't make any sense. Trying to get around this problem by placing r in unevaluation quotes won't work, but a simple remedy is shown at the end of the next section.

2.17 Sets and Lists

Enclosing a sequence in braces {} produces a set. In the next example, E is assigned the empty set as its value, and S is assigned the set containing the elements *apple*, *orange* and *pear*.

```
> E := {} ;
```
$$E := \{ \}$$

```
> S := { apple , orange , pear } ;
```
$$S := \{apple, orange, pear\}$$

Maple may rearrange the entries in a set, and will delete repeated elements.

```
> T := { 2 , 3 , 1 , 3 , 2 , 1 } ;
```
$$T := \{1, 2, 3\}$$

Set-theoretic operations can be performed using `union`, `intersect` and `minus` to represent $\cup$, $\cap$ and $\backslash$, respectively.

```
> S := { 1 , 2 , 3 } :
> T := { 3 , 4 , 5 } :
> S union T ;
```
$$\{1, 2, 3, 4, 5\}$$

```
> S intersect T ;
```
$$\{3\}$$

```
> S minus { 2 } ;
```
$$\{1, 3\}$$

Some care is needed with tests for subsets, because the `subset` keyword actually represents $\subseteq$, rather than $\subset$.

```
> S := { 1 , 2 } :
> { 2 } subset S ;
```
$$true$$

```
> { 1 , 2 } subset S ;
```
$$true$$

A test for a proper subset (i.e. $\subset$) can be applied as follows.

```
> S := { 1 , 2 } :
> ( { 1 , 2 } subset S ) and not ( { 1 , 2 } = S ) ;
```
$$false$$

Excessive typing can be avoided by defining a functional operator to perform this test (see Section 3.4) if it is needed frequently.

★ Under some circumstances, repeated elements will not be deleted from a set of vectors, matrices, arrays or tables. See Section 5.8 for an explanation.

Square brackets [ ] can be used to construct lists; an empty pair of square brackets produces the empty list. The order of entries in a list is preserved, and repeated elements are not deleted.

```
> A := [ 4 , 7 , 2 , 17 , 12 , 7 ] ;
```
$$A := [4, 7, 2, 17, 12, 7]$$

Lists have many uses in Maple, but they are immutable, meaning they cannot be changed after they have been created. Any apparently successful attempt to change a list actually creates a new list. Where changes to entries are needed, arrays (see Section 7.5) offer much greater efficiency.

★ Sequences, lists and sets can contain entries which are themselves lists or sets. For example, lists of lists can be used to construct matrices (see Chapter 5) and in creating certain types of plot (see Chapter 6).

Most statements (but not assignments) can be enclosed in braces or square brackets. The result is then a set or a list, respectively.

```
> { Pi , evalf( Pi ) } ;
```
$$\{3.141592654, \pi\}$$

```
> [ cos( 0 ) , cos( Pi / 2 ) , cos( Pi ) ] ;
```
$$[1, 0, -1]$$

```
> { solve( x^2 + 4 * x + 4 = 0 ) } ;
```
$$\{-2\}$$

```
> [ solve( x^2 + 4 * x + 4 = 0 ) ] ;
```
$$[-2, -2]$$

The last two statements each determine the roots of the quadratic equation $x^2 + 4x + 4 = 0$ using the **solve** command (see Chapter 4 for more about this). When the result is converted into a set, one instance of the repeated root at $x = -2$ is deleted.

The sequence of entries (operands) can be extracted from a list or set using the **op** command (an empty selection operator can also be used; see Section 2.18).

```
> S := { a , b , c } :
```

```
> op( S ) ;
```

$$a, b, c$$

```
> L := [ 1 , 2 , 3 ] :
> op( L ) ;
```

$$1, 2, 3$$

There are many Maple commands that perform operations on sets and lists. For example, `numelems` counts the number of elements, and `member` determines whether a list or set contains a particular object.

```
> s := { a , b , c } :
> numelems( s ) ;
```

$$3$$

```
> member( a , s ) ;
```

true

```
> L := [ 1 , 0 , 3 , 2 ] :
> numelems( L ) ;
```

$$4$$

```
> member( 4 , L ) ;
```

false

An alternative way to check membership is to use the `in` operator with `evalb`.

```
> G := [ 5 , 6 , 2 ] :
> evalb( 5 in G ) ;
```

true

To make these commands work with sequences, simply convert to lists using square brackets.

```
> Q := alpha , beta , gamma :
> numelems( [ Q ] ) ;
```

$$3$$

```
> member( beta , [ Q ] ) ;
```

true

```
> evalb( delta in [ Q ] ) ;
```

$$false$$

Section 2.19 explains how to apply operations to each entry in a sequence, set or list individually.

2.18 Indices

Indices can be denoted using square brackets, so where we might write A_j to mean 'the jth entry in the sequence A', in Maple notation we use A[j].

```
> A := 1 , 8 , 27 , 64 , 125 ;
```

$$A := 1, 8, 27, 64, 125$$

```
> A[3] ;
```

$$27$$

The same syntax also works with lists and sets.

```
> L := [ 4 , 7 , 2 , 17 , 12 , 7 ] :
> L[4] ;
```

$$17$$

```
> S := { orange , apple , pear } ;
```

$$S := \{apple, orange, pear\}$$

```
> S[1] ;
```

$$apple$$

Attempting to access an element that is out of range results in an error.

```
> A := { 4 , 7 , 2 } :
> A[4] ;
Error, invalid subscript selector
```

Indices can also be used to access characters in a string.

```
> s := "abc" :
> s[3] ;
```

$$"c"$$

In this case, using an out of range index produces an empty string.

```
> s := "def" ;
```

$$s := \text{"def"}$$

```
> s[4] ;
```

$$\text{""}$$

Naively, it may appear that assignments can be made to the entries in a short list using indices.

```
> L := [ 1 , 2 , 3 ] ;
```

$$L := [1, 2, 3]$$

```
> L[2] := a :
> L ;
```

$$[1, a, 3]$$

However, the effect of this is to create a new list which replaces the old one, so such operations are very inefficient. For this reason, using indices to change the entries in a long list is forbidden, and will result in an error. In situations where changes to entries are needed, arrays should be used instead (see Section 7.5).

An index undergoes full evaluation, even in the context of evaluation to a name. This includes indices that appear on the left-hand side of assignments. In the next example, A[j] refers to the third entry in the list A, despite the fact that A_j is itself a valid name.

```
> A := [ 4 , 7 , 2 , 17 , 12 , 7 ] :
> j := 3 :
> evaln( A[j] ) ;   # Evaluate to a name
```

$$A_3$$

```
> % ;
```

$$2$$

```
> A[j] := 43 :
> A ;
```

$$A := [4, 7, 43, 17, 12, 7] :$$

A sequence of indices can be used to access the individual elements in a list of lists (or set of sets, etc.).

```
> L := [ [ 0 , 1 ] , [ a , b ] , [ pi , eta , mu ] ] ;
```

$$L := [[0, 1], [a, b], [\pi, \eta, \mu]]$$

```
> L[2] ;
```

$$[a, b]$$

```
> L[2,1] ;
```

$$a$$

The *range operator* .. can be used to access multiple consecutive elements of a list, set, sequence or string. The result of such an operation has the same type as the original object, so using a range to access part of a list produces a new list, etc.

```
> A := [ 4 , 7 , 2 , 17 , 12 , 7 ] :
> A[1..3] ;
```

$$[4, 7, 2]$$

```
> s := "abcdef" ;
```

$$s := \text{"abcdef"}$$

```
> s[2..4] ;
```

$$\text{"bcd"}$$

Omitting the beginning of the range causes Maple to start from the first element, and omitting the last causes it to continue until the end.

```
> A := [ 4 , 7 , 2 , 17 , 12 , 7 ] :
> A[..4] ;
```

$$[4, 7, 2, 17]$$

```
> A[2..] ;
```

$$[7, 2, 17, 12, 7]$$

Consequently, A[..] returns a copy of A. This is not very useful with lists or sets but it can be used to extract a whole row or column from a matrix (see Section 5.2). In contrast, an empty selection operator extracts the elements of a set or list, returning the entries in a sequence.

```
> C := { larch , chestnut , birch } ;
```

$$C := \{birch, chestnut, larch\}$$

```
> C[] ;
```

birch, chestnut, larch

Maple also permits the use of negative indices. For a list, set or sequence *L*, L[-1] always refers to the last entry, L[-2] to the penultimate entry, etc.

```
> L := [ a , b , c , d ] :
> L[-1] ;
```

d

Negative indices can appear in ranges, but the entries must still be traversed from left to right. Trying to go in the opposite direction will result in an empty structure, or an error. In the next example, L[-2..2] attempts to access the entries of the list *L* in the wrong direction, but L[2..-2] works because it selects from the second entry to the penultimate entry.

```
> L := [ sheep , pig , cow , llama , goat ] ;
```

$$L := [sheep, pig, cow, llama, goat]$$

```
> L[-2..2] ;
Error, invalid subscript selector
> L[2..-2] ;
```

[*pig, cow, llama*]

Negative indices can be used in the same way with matrices and vectors, but some care is needed if they are used with arrays (see Section 7.5).

2.19 Element-wise Operations

Maple allows operations to be applied to each element of a list or set in a single statement. This also applies to matrices and vectors (see Chapter 5), arrays (Section 7.5) and tables (Section 7.6). Element-wise operations are indicated by appending a tilde symbol ~ to an operator or command. In the next example, L^2 refers to the square of the list *L* (whatever that means), but the tilde symbol in the last statement causes each individual element to be squared and placed in a new list.

```
> L := [ 1 , 2 , 3 ] :
> L^2 ;
```

$$[1, 2, 3]^2$$

```
> L^~ 2 ;
```

$$[1, 4, 9]$$

Similarly, one cannot take the cosine of a list, but it is possible to take the cosine of each individual element.

```
> S := [ 0 , Pi / 2 , Pi ] :
> cos( S )
Error, invalid input: cos expects its 1st argument, x, to
be of type algebraic, but received [0, (1/2)*Pi, Pi]
> cos~( S ) ;
```

$$[1, 0, -1]$$

An element-wise operation can also be used to perform arithmetic operations on corresponding entries in two lists or sets of equal size.

```
> L := [ 1 , 2 , 3 ] :
> M := [ 4 , 6 , 8 ] :
> M *~ L ;
```

$$[4, 12, 24]$$

Some element-wise operations don't actually require a tilde symbol, but they still work if it is present.

```
> L := [ 0 , Pi / 2 , Pi ] :
> evalf( L ) ;
```

$$[0., 1.570796327, 3.141592654]$$

```
> evalf~( L ) ;
```

$$[0., 1.570796327, 3.141592654]$$

Unfortunately, there doesn't seem to be any underlying logic that determines which commands work without a tilde symbol, and which don't. Therefore, as a general rule it is best to always include the tilde to indicate an element-wise operation, unless the operation is mathematically defined in an element-wise fashion (e.g. vector and matrix addition, and multiplication by scalars). In this case Maple respects the definition without a tilde symbol; to do otherwise would be absurd.

It is possible to apply some, but not all, element-wise operations to sequences. Typically, only arithmetic operators will work. This is because commands generally expect a sequence of arguments, and when combined with an element-wise operation this leads to ambiguity.

```
> S := -Pi , 0 , Pi :
> S^~ 2 ;
```

$$\pi^2, 0, \pi^2$$

```
> y := 1 :
> x := 0 , 1 , sqrt( 3 ) :
> arctan~( y , x ) ;
Error, (in arctan) expecting 1 or 2 arguments, got 4
```

Trying to allow for element-wise operations with sequences in cases such as this would be more trouble than it is worth; the simple remedy is to convert the sequence into a list using square brackets.

```
> y := 1 :
> x := 0 , 1 , sqrt( 3 ) :
> arctan~( y , [ x ] ) ;
```

$$\left[\frac{1}{2} \pi, \frac{1}{4} \pi, \frac{1}{6} \pi \right]$$

★ Maple allows names to start with a tilde symbol (without name quotes), so a statement such as M *~L is potentially misleading; it actually means M *~ L, but it could be mistaken for M * ~L. Parentheses can be used to disambiguate such constructions, but spaces are usually sufficient.

★ In older versions of Maple, it was necessary to use the map and map2 commands for element-wise operations. For most purposes the tilde symbol is simpler and clearer, but map and map2 still have some uses, because their behaviour is different from ~ in certain cases. Execute ?map for more details (see also ?elementwise).

2.20 The seq, add and mul Commands

The seq command is used to generate sequences. Often this is more concise than manually entering the terms.

```
> seq( j^2 , j = 1 .. 10 ) ;
```
$$1, 4, 9, 16, 25, 36, 49, 64, 81, 100$$

```
> seq( x^p , p = 1 .. 5 ) ;
```
$$x, x^2, x^3, x^4, x^5$$

```
> L := [ 2, 4, 6, 8, 10 ] ;
```
$$L := [2, 4, 6, 8, 10]$$

```
> seq( L[q] , q = 3 .. 5 ) ;
```
$$6, 8, 10$$

```
> seq( j , j = 0 .. 10 , 2 ) ;
```
$$0, 2, 4, 6, 8, 10$$

Note the third argument used to obtain a non-unit step size in the last statement (`seq( 2 * j , j = 0 .. 5`) could also be used). It is also possible to generate a sequence of letters from the alphabet. The default behaviour is then to step forward one letter at a time, but a third argument can be used to request a different increment, as before.

```
> seq( c , c = "a" .. "g" ) ;
```
$$\text{"a", "b", "c", "d", "e", "f", "g"}$$

```
> seq( c , c = "g" .. "a" , -1 ) ;
```
$$\text{"g", "f", "e", "d", "c", "b", "a"}$$

```
> seq( c , c = "a" .. "z" , 3 ) ;
```
$$\text{"a", "d", "g", "j", "m", "p", "s", "v", "y"}$$

In versions up to Maple 18, the `in` operator was used to generate a sequence of all the elements contained in a larger object, such as a sequence, string, vector or matrix (see Chapter 5), or an array (see Section 7.5). However, this is rarely needed in Maple 2015 and later.

```
> seq( "pig" ) ;   # Maple 2015 & later
```
$$\text{"p", "i", "g"}$$

```
> seq( u , u in "pig" ) ;
```
$$\text{"p", "i", "g"}$$

```
> v := < 2 , 0 , 9 > ;   # Creates a vector
```

$$v := \begin{bmatrix} 2 \\ 0 \\ 9 \end{bmatrix}$$

```
> seq( v ) ;   # Maple 2015 & later
```

$$2, 0, 9$$

```
> seq( x , x in v ) ;
```

$$2, 0, 9$$

In the next example, the **in** operator is used to obtain a sequence by squaring all the entries in the list L.

```
> L := [ 6 , 2 , 5 , 7 ] :
> seq( c^2 , c in L ) ;
```

$$36, 4, 25, 49$$

In Maple 2015 and later, this can also be achieved using an element-wise operation (see Section 2.19).

```
> L := [ 6 , 2 , 5 , 7 ] :
> seq( L^~ 2 ) ;   # Maple 2015 & later
```

$$36, 4, 25, 49$$

The **add** command can be used to sum a finite number of numerical values. It has much the same syntax as **seq**, and should not be confused with the **sum** command, which attempts summation of series using analytic and approximate methods (see Section 3.6).

```
> add( j^2 , j = 1 .. 10 ) ;
```

$$385$$

```
> L := [ 1 , 2 , 3 , 4 , 5 ] ;
```

$$L := [1, 2, 3, 4, 5];$$

```
> add( L[j] , j = 3 .. 5 ) ;
```

$$12$$

```
> add( L ) ;   # Maple 2015 & later
```

$$15$$

```
> add( p , p in L ) ;
```
$$15$$

Similarly, the `mul` command can be used to multiply a sequence of values.

```
> mul( j^2 , j = 2 .. 10 ) ;
```
$$13168189440000$$
```
> S := 4 , 7 , 2 , 9 ;
```
$$S := 4, 7, 2, 9$$
```
> mul( S[j] , j = 1 .. 3 )
```
$$56$$
```
> mul( S^~ 2 ) ;  # Maple 2015 & later
```
$$254016$$
```
> mul( c^2 , c in S ) ;
```
$$254016$$

Arguments passed to **seq**, **add** and **mul** are subject to special evaluation rules. The index is not affected by prior assignments, and has its old value (if any) restored after the command has been executed.

```
> q := Pi :
> seq( q^3 , q = 1 .. 5 ) ;
```
$$1, 8, 27, 64, 125$$
```
> q ;
```
$$\pi$$
```
> L := [ 27 , 42 , 99 , -1 , 17 ] :
> add( q , q in L ) ;
```
$$184$$
```
> q ;
```
$$\pi$$

The process of executing a **seq**, **add** or **mul** command with two or three arguments is as follows. First, Maple determines the index variable and assigns its initial value, using the second argument (parts of which may need to be evaluated). Only now is the first argument evaluated. Subsequent terms are generated by updating the index (using the third argument if it is present), and evaluating the first argument again. This is illustrated by the next example, which works because *j* is assigned a value from the range $1, \ldots, 5$ *before* Maple attempts to evaluate `evalf[ j ]( Pi )`.

```
> seq( evalf[ j ]( Pi ) , j = 1 .. 5 ) ;
```

$$3., 3.1, 3.14, 3.142, 3.1416$$

Using a symbol to specify the number of significant digits required would result in an error.

2.21 Types

When performing simple mathematical calculations with Maple, it is rarely necessary to distinguish between different types of data such as real and complex numbers. However, there are many situations where this is important. A complete list of the types available can be obtained by executing `?type`, and the `whattype` command can be used to determine the type of a given object.

```
> whattype( 1 ) ;
```

$$integer$$

```
> whattype( 3.2 ) ;
```

$$float$$

The result returned by `whattype` is the *basic type* of the argument, but it should be noted that objects in Maple can also have one or more subtypes. The `type` command can be used to test whether an expression is of a given type.

```
> type( 1 , integer ) ;
```

$$true$$

```
> type( 1 , numeric ) ;
```

$$true$$

```
> type( 1 , complex ) ;
```

$$true$$

For lists and sets, we can check either the type of the container object, or the types of both the container and its elements. In the latter case, the test will return *true* only if all of the elements match the specified type.

```
> L := [ 1 , 2 , 3 ] :
> S := { a , 2 , 3 } :
> type( L , list ) ;
```

$$true$$

```
> type( L , list( numeric ) ) ;
```

$$true$$

```
> type( S , set( numeric ) ) ;
```

$$false$$

However, this does not work with sequences.

```
> s := 1 , 2 , 3 :
> whattype( s ) ;
```

$$exprseq$$

```
> type( s , exprseq ) ;
Error, invalid input: type expects 2 arguments, but
received 4
```

When the last statement is executed, s is evaluated to $1, 2, 3$ before being passed to **type**, which expects only two arguments but now receives four. Attempting to avoid this problem using unevaluation quotes fails because there is actually no sequence type in Maple.

```
> s := 1 , 2 , 3 :
> type( 's' , exprseq ) ;
Error, type `exprseq` does not exist
```

Another technical issue arises when a type shares its name with a command. For example, there is a **Matrix** type, and a command **Matrix**, which can be used to construct matrices (see Chapter 5 for details).

```
> M := Matrix( 2 , 2 ) ;
```

$$M := \begin{bmatrix} 0 & 0 \\ 0 & 0 \end{bmatrix}$$

```
> type( M , Matrix ) ;
```

$$true$$

```
> type( M , Matrix( numeric ) ) ;
Error, (in Matrix) dimension parameters are required for
this form of initializer
```

Here, the test to determine whether *M* is a matrix succeeds, but the second test fails because arguments undergo prior evaluation before being passed to the **type** command, and **Matrix(numeric)** is not a valid use of the **Matrix** command. The solution is to use unevaluation quotes.

```
> M := Matrix( 2 , 2 ) ;
```

$$M := \begin{bmatrix} 0 & 0 \\ 0 & 0 \end{bmatrix}$$

```
> type( M , 'Matrix( numeric )' ) ;
```

$$true$$

The same issue affects vectors and also arrays (Section 7.5).

An alternative syntax for testing types uses the *type operator* : :. This is similar to a relational operator in that **evalb** must be used to cause the query to evaluate to either *true* or *false*.

```
> evalb( I :: integer ) ;
```

$$false$$

```
> evalb( I :: complex ) ;
```

$$true$$

```
> evalb( [ 1 , 2 , 3 ] :: list( numeric ) ) ;
```

$$true$$

```
> M := Matrix( 2 , 2 ) ;
```

$$M := \begin{bmatrix} 0 & 0 \\ 0 & 0 \end{bmatrix}$$

```
> evalb( M :: 'Matrix( numeric )' ) ;
```

$$true$$

2.22 Packages

Maple's facilities can be extended by loading packages, which define additional commands. The packages discussed here are provided as standard with Maple. There are also paid-for add-on products called toolboxes, which should not be confused with packages. To load a package, use the `with` command.

```
> with( LinearAlgebra ) :
```

In general, each package need only be loaded once in a worksheet, but issuing a `restart` command (or closing and reopening) will remove any packages that have been loaded. Packages can also be removed using `unwith`.

```
> unwith( LinearAlgebra ) :
```

It is possible to access package commands without loading via `with`. The next example shows two methods that can be used to obtain all possible permutations of the list $[a, b, c]$, without the need to load the `combinat` package, which provides the necessary command. The first syntax is universal, whereas the *member selection operator* `:-` does not work with some older packages.

```
> combinat[ permute ]( [ a , b , c ] ) ;
```
$$[[a, b, c], [a, c, b], [b, a, c], [b, c, a], [c, a, b], [c, b, a]]$$

```
> combinat :- permute( [ a , b , c ] ) ;
```
$$[[a, b, c], [a, c, b], [b, a, c], [b, c, a], [c, a, b], [c, b, a]]$$

One reason to use this method is to avoid situations in which packages conflict with each other by creating commands with identical names, but different behaviour. This is relatively rare, but an example occurs in Section 5.5.

Some packages contain subpackages, which can be accessed by loading the parent package first. The next example loads `EscapeTime`, which is a subpackage of the `Fractals` package.

```
> with( Fractals ) :
> with( EscapeTime ) :
```

Alternatively, a subpackage can be loaded directly, without loading anything else from the parent package. Executing the following statement loads the **Basics** component of the **Student** package only.

```
> with( Student[ Basics ] ) :
```

★ To see a list of commands and subpackages provided by a package, use a semicolon to terminate the **with** command.

★ If Maple unexpectedly returns a statement unevaluated, check that all necessary packages have been loaded.

```
> fibonacci( 10 ) ;   # 10th Fibonacci number
```
$$fibonacci(10)$$
```
> with( combinat ) :   # Load the combinatorics package
> fibonacci( 10 ) ;    # Try again...
```
$$55$$

★ To open the help page for a package command, it is sometimes necessary to give the package name as the topic and the command as the subtopic (see Section 2.2). For example **?point** leads to a mathematical definition of a point in Maple 18, and to a description of different units used for measuring angles in Maple 2015 and 2016. On the other hand **?plottools,point** leads to the help page for the **point** command, which is part of the **plottools** package.

Many of the packages provided with Maple are likely to be useful to small subsets of users, and some are intended for advanced users only. Nevertheless, it is important to be aware that a very wide range of features is available. To give an indication of this, a selection of the most widely used packages is listed here, along with brief details of what each of them contains. We also mention some more esoteric packages that offer features one might not expect to find in Maple. A small number of packages have been deprecated, and replaced by newer packages. These include **group**, **linalg**, **networks**, **numtheory**, **stats** and **student** (with a lower case 's'). A complete list of all available packages, along with details of deprecated packages and their replacements can be obtained using **?index,package**.

Mathematical Extensions

- `combinat`
  Combinatoric functions, including permutations, combinations and partitions.
- `CurveFitting`
  Commands for fitting functions through (or close to) data.
- `DETools`
  Extends the features available for working with ordinary differential equations.
- `GraphTheory`
  Commands for creating and manipulating graphs, meaning sets of vertices (or nodes) connected by edges. For graphs of functions or data, see Chapter 6.
- `LinearAlgebra`
  Extends the facilities available for working with vectors and matrices. See Chapter 5 for details of some features provided by this package.
- `NumberTheory`
  Provides commands for investigating the properties of natural numbers and integers.
- `PDETools`
  Commands for analytically solving partial differential equations.
- `SolveTools`
  Commands for solving systems of equations. This package is used internally by the `solve` command (see Chapter 4) but it can also be used directly to instruct Maple to use a particular solving method. This can lead to greater efficiency in some cases (e.g. where a system of equations is known to be linear). However, direct use of `SolveTools` is recommended only for advanced users.
- `Statistics`
  Commands for statistics and data analysis.
- `SumTools`
  Commands for summing series. This package is used internally by the `sum` command (see Section 3.6). Beyond this its facilities are largely intended for advanced users. However, the `Telescoping` command (which is part of the `DefiniteSum` subpackage) is used in Section 3.6.

- `VectorCalculus`

  Vector calculus operations such as divergence and curl, and line and surface integrals.

Graphics Extensions

- `Fractals`

  Commands for creating and manipulating fractals.

- `ImageTools`

  Advanced commands for image processing.

- `plots`

  Extends the features available for visualising mathematical structures. See Chapter 6 for a discussion of some features provided by this package.

- `plottools`

  Facilities for drawing basic graphical objects such as arrows, circles and spheres. See Sections 6.5 and 6.7 for examples that use this package.

Programming Facilities

- `CodeTools`

  Facilities for optimising Maple code.

- `FileTools`

  Commands for manipulating external files.

- `Grid`

  Facilities for parallel programming, using a cluster or network.

- `LibraryTools`

  Enables storage of Maple code in user-defined libraries. Code stored in this way can be used from different worksheets without the need to create multiple copies. This is very useful for large projects.

- `Threads`

  Commands for parallel programming, using a computer with multiple CPUs.

Interacting with Other Software and Languages

- `CodeGeneration`

  Translation tools for converting Maple code into other programming languages, including C, Fortran, Matlab, Perl and Python.

- `ExcelTools`

  Import and export facilities for reading from, and writing to, Excel spreadsheets.

- `Matlab`

  Provides a set of commands that form the 'Matlab link'. These send commands and other information from Maple to Matlab (provided this is available) and retrieve results. Also provides facilities for translating Matlab code into Maple code.

- `MMaTranslator`

  Translation tools for converting Mathematica expressions and files into their Maple equivalents.

Programming the Maple Interface

- `ContextMenu`

  Allows users to customise the effect of right-clicking on a Maple expression.

- `DocumentTools`

  Commands for programming embedded objects such as buttons, palettes and slider bars in Maple worksheets.

- `Maplets`

  Commands for creating graphical user interface elements such as message windows and dialogue boxes. Using this package, it is possible to create demonstration worksheets that users can operate without the need for expertise in Maple.

Miscellaneous

- `AudioTools`

  Facilities for reading and writing WAVE audio files, and for performing basic audio processing.

- CUDA
  Enables the use of graphics hardware to accelerate linear algebra routines. At the time of writing, this seems to be at an early stage of development, and only one operation (matrix multiplication) is supported. The `external_calling` command, which can be used to invoke procedures written in C or Fortran from within Maple, is likely to provide a better option for dealing with very large linear systems containing numerical data.
- Student
  Designed to assist students in learning standard undergraduate mathematics, this package provides facilities for displaying step by step calculations and visualising mathematical concepts.
- Units
  Commands for converting physical quantities between different unit systems.
- URL
  Commands for sending and receiving data over a network using universal resource locators (URLs).

3

Algebra and Calculus

This chapter introduces some of Maple's symbolic computation facilities. Many of the commands discussed have apparently self-explanatory purposes; for example `simplify` simplifies its argument, `expand` expands and `factor` factorises. However, a word of warning is in order here: commands may not always produce the result you expect. This is because the precise meaning of terms such as 'factorise' can be ambiguous: should quadratic terms with complex roots be factorised, or left as they are? Are approximate roots acceptable? If so, how accurate do they need to be? What if the exact expressions for the roots are more than a page long? The answers to questions such as these may be obvious to you (and perhaps to other human mathematicians), but they usually come from the wider context of the problem, about which Maple knows nothing. Consequently, it is often necessary to supply algebraic manipulation commands with optional arguments to coerce Maple into producing the results you need.

★ Always tell Maple exactly what you want. Otherwise you may end up with something different.

★ It is possible to perform some operations by right-clicking on Maple output and selecting an option from the resulting context menu. Maple will automatically insert the appropriate command and will reference the output using an equation label (see Section 2.3).

★ Do not rely on a context menu if the statement it produces is unfamiliar. Doing so can lead to extreme frustration if the operation fails or produces an unexpected result.

3.1 Manipulating Expressions

The `factor` command is used to factorise polynomials. By default, Maple factorises in terms of coefficients of the same type as those in the original expression. In the next example, the polynomial has integer coefficients, so only one root (the integer) is obtained.

```
> factor( x^3 - x^2 + 3 * x + 5 ) ;
```
$$(x + 1)(x^2 - 2x + 5)$$

A second argument can be provided to extend the field over which the factorisation is sought.

```
> factor( x^3 - x^2 + 3 * x + 5 , I ) ;
```
$$-(x + 1)(-x + 1 + 2\,I)(x - 1 + 2\,I)$$

More than one such extension can be supplied in a list or a set.

```
> factor( x^2 + 2 , [ sqrt( 2 ) , I ] ) ;
```
$$-\left(I\sqrt{2} - x\right)\left(I\sqrt{2} + x\right)$$

Another possibility is to supply the `complex` option to the `factor` command. This causes Maple to factorise fully, but it will produce a floating point result, even if all of the roots are actually integers.

```
> factor( x^3 - x^2 + 3 * x + 5 , complex ) ;
```
$$(x + 1.00000000000000)(x - 1. + 2.\,I)(x - 1. - 2.\,I)$$

```
> factor( x^3 - 6 * x^2 + 11 * x - 6 , complex ) ;
```
$$(x - 1.00000000000000)(x - 2.00000000000000)$$
$$(x - 3.00000000000000)$$

Here Maple has switched to hardware arithmetic (see Section 2.8), so the answer is displayed with 15 significant digits. Obtaining an exact factorisation without knowing which extensions to supply requires some trickery, but it is possible; see Section 4.1.

The `expand` command is used to expand out brackets (for series expansions, see Section 3.9). It can also be used to apply well-known mathematical rules such as addition formulae and double angle formulae.

```
> expand( ( x + 1 )^2 ) ;
```
$$x^2 + 2x + 1$$

```
> expand( sin( x + y ) ) ;
```
$$\sin(x)\cos(y) + \cos(x)\sin(y)$$
```
> expand( tanh( 2 * x ) ) ;
```
$$\frac{2\sinh(x)\cosh(x)}{2\cosh(x)^2 - 1}$$

To prevent one or more subexpressions from being expanded, a sequence of optional arguments can be passed to **expand**. In the next example, it is obvious that expanding the brackets in the first term will lead to simplification, but nothing is gained by applying addition formulae to $\sin(x + y)$ and e^{x-y}, so this is prevented.

```
> S := ( ( x - 1 )^2 - ( x + 1 )^2 )
                        * sin( x + y ) * exp( x - y ) ;
```
$$S := ((x - 1)^2 - (x + 1)^2)\sin(x + y)e^{x-y}$$
```
> expand( S , x + y , x - y ) ;
```
$$-4\sin(x + y)e^{x-y}x$$

The little known command **frontend** can be used to multiply out brackets but perform no other expansions. Full details of **frontend** are beyond the scope of this book (see **?frontend**), but the syntax for expansion is shown in the next example.

```
> S := ( ( x - y )^2 - ( x + y )^2 )
                        * sin( x + y ) * exp( x - y ) ;
```
$$S := ((x - y)^2 - (x + y)^2)\sin(x + y)e^{x-y}$$
```
> frontend( expand , [ S ] ) ;
```
$$-4\sin(x + y)e^{x-y}xy$$

Note the difference between this and the previous example: preventing expansion of $\sin(x + y)$ and e^{x-y} by passing the optional arguments **x + y** and **x - y** to **expand** would also prevent expansion of $(x - y)^2$ and $(x + y)^2$ (of course **sin(x + y)** and **exp(x - y)** could be used as the optional arguments instead).

★ Commands can be combined to reduce the need for ditto operators (or temporary variables) at intermediate steps.

```
> f := ( x - sqrt( 1 + x ) )^4
                    + ( x + sqrt( 1 + x ) )^4 - 2 ;
```
$$f := \left(x - \sqrt{1+x}\right)^4 + \left(x + \sqrt{1+x}\right)^4 - 2$$

```
> expand( f ) ;  # or expand( % )
```
$$2x^4 + 12x^3 + 14x^2 + 4x$$

```
> factor( % ) ;
```
$$2x(x+1)(x^2+5x+2)$$

```
> factor( expand( f ) ) ;  # Do it all at once
```
$$2x(x+1)(x^2+5x+2)$$

In most cases, Maple simplifies expressions without assistance, but it does miss some possibilities. The **simplify** command encourages it to try harder.

```
> ( 1 + t )^5 - ( 1 - t )^5 ;
```
$$(1+t)^5 - (1-t)^5$$

```
> simplify( % ) ;
```
$$2t^5 + 20t^3 + 10t$$

```
> cos( x )^2 + sin( x )^2 ;
```
$$\cos(x)^2 + \sin(x)^2$$

```
> simplify( % ) ;
```
$$1$$

```
> 4^(1/2) ;
```
$$\sqrt{4}$$

```
> simplify( % ) ;
```
$$2$$

★ **sqrt(4)** evaluates to 2 without the **simplify** command. This is one reason to prefer **sqrt** over **^(1/2)**.

Maple is *careful* when it performs simplifications involving square roots.

```
> simplify( sqrt( x^2 ) ) ;
```
$$\text{csgn}(x)\, x$$

Here the complex sign function, which is defined as

$$\mathrm{csgn}(x) = \begin{cases} 1 & \text{if } -\dfrac{\pi}{2} < \arg(x) \le \dfrac{\pi}{2}, \\ -1 & \text{otherwise}, \end{cases}$$

appears because x could be complex (or negative). To ignore such possibilities, use the **symbolic** option.

```
> simplify( sqrt( x^2 ) , symbolic ) ;
```

$$x$$

Another method is to instruct Maple to make an assumption.

```
> sqrt( x^2 ) assuming( x > 0 ) ;
```

$$x$$

See Section 3.10 for more about assumptions.

In many cases, there is no accepted 'simplest' form of an expression; different forms may be easier to use for different tasks. In these circumstances, commands with precisely defined effects are to be preferred. For example, **normal** puts an expression over a common denominator. With the **expanded** option, it also multiplies out the brackets in the denominator.

```
> P := 1 / ( 1 + x ) - 1 / ( 1 - x ) ;
```

$$P := \frac{1}{1+x} - \frac{1}{-x+1}$$

```
> normal( P ) ;
```

$$\frac{2x}{(1+x)(x-1)}$$

```
> normal( P , expanded ) ;
```

$$\frac{2x}{x^2-1}$$

The **convert** command can be used to go in the opposite direction, and split expressions into partial fractions.

```
> convert( 1 / ( x^2 - 1 ) , parfrac ) ;
```

$$\frac{1}{2(x-1)} - \frac{1}{2(x+1)}$$

```
> Q := ( tan( x ) + x ) / ( x * tan( x ) ) ;
```

$$Q := \frac{\tan(x) + x}{x \tan(x)}$$

```
> convert( Q , parfrac ) ;
```

$$\frac{1}{x} + \frac{1}{\tan(x)}$$

★ It is sometimes necessary to apply the `simplify` or `expand` command before checking whether two expressions are equal.

```
> evalb( ( a + b )^2 = a^2 + b^2 + 2 * a * b ) ;
```

false

```
> evalb( expand( ( a + b )^2 )
                    = a^2 + b^2 + 2 * a * b ) ;
```

true

```
> evalb( ( a + b )^2 - ( a^2 + b^2 + 2 * a * b ) = 0 ) ;
```

false

```
> evalb( simplify( ( a + b )^2
                - ( a^2 + b^2 + 2 * a * b ) ) = 0 ) ;
```

true

★ It can be difficult to force Maple to display an expression in a particular form. To check your own answer to a problem it is usually best to subtract it from Maple's answer and apply `simplify` to the result.

3.2 Extracting Parts of an Expression

The `collect` command is used to arrange an expression into coefficients multiplied by powers of a given quantity. Subsequently, the `coeff` command can be used to extract the coefficients. In the next example, an expression is arranged into powers of x, and the coefficient of each power is obtained.

```
> p := expand( ( x + y + z )^2 ) ;
```

$$p := x^2 + 2xy + 2xz + y^2 + 2yz + z^2$$

```
> q := collect( p , x ) ;
```

$$q := x^2 + (2y + 2z)x + 2yz + z^2 + y^2$$

```
> coeff( q , x , 2 ) ;
```
$$1$$

```
> coeff( q , x , 1 ) ;
```
$$2y + 2z$$

```
> coeff( q , x , 0 ) ;
```
$$2yz + z^2 + y^2$$

It is also possible the collect the coefficients of more complex expressions.

```
> f := 2 * exp( x ) + 4 + x * exp( x ) ;
```
$$f := 2e^x + 4 + xe^x$$

```
> collect( f , exp( x ) ) ;
```
$$4 + (x + 2)e^x$$

```
> coeff( % , exp( x ) , 1 ) ;
```
$$x + 2$$

The **numer** and **denom** commands can be used to extract the numerator and denominator from a fraction.

```
> f := ( x + 1 ) / ( x - 1 ) ;
```
$$f := \frac{x + 1}{x - 1}$$

```
> numer( f ) ;
```
$$x + 1$$

A note of caution: the terms 'numerator' and 'denominator' are not well-defined for an expression that does not consist of a single fraction. Using **numer** and **denom** in such cases can have surprising results.

```
> a := 1 / x - ( 2 * x + 1 ) / x^2 ;
```
$$a := \frac{1}{x} - \frac{2x + 1}{x^2}$$

```
> numer( a ) ;
```
$$-x - 1$$

```
> denom( a ) ;
```

$$x^2$$

Here, Maple puts the expression over a common denominator and
simplifies as far as possible before finding the numerator and denominator.
However, it won't always do this. In the next example, the results share a
common factor of x, which one might reasonably expect to be cancelled.

```
> b := 1 / x^3 - ( 1 - x + x^2 ) / x^3 ;
```

$$b := \frac{1}{x^3} - \frac{1 - x + x^2}{x^3}$$

```
> numer( b ) ;
```

$$-x(x - 1)$$

```
> denom( b ) ;
```

$$x^3$$

In general, the safest approach is to apply the **normal** command to an
expression before using **numer** or **denom**.

```
> b := normal( 1 / x^3 - ( 1 - x + x^2 ) / x^3 ) ;
```

$$-\frac{x - 1}{x^2}$$

```
> numer( b ) ;
```

$$-x + 1$$

```
> denom( b ) ;
```

$$x^2$$

The **op** command can be used to select a particular operand (term) from
an arbitrary expression. This must be used with extreme care, because
the order in which terms appear can vary, and exactly what constitutes a
'term' is not obvious in all cases.

```
> f := a + b + c :
> op( 1 , f ) ;
```

$$a$$

```
> p := ( x + 2 ) * ( x - 1 ) * ( x - 2 ) :
```

```
> op( 2 , p ) ;
```

$$x - 1$$

```
> q := ( 2 * x ) * ( x + 2 ) :
> op( 1 , q ) ;
```

$$2$$

The last result arises because the parentheses around $2 * x$ are removed during automatic simplification (which does not change the expression). Consequently, Maple considers the first operand of q to be 2.

★ Only use op to select terms if you can see the result it produces; do not use this method in an automated worksheet.

3.3 Substitutions

There are two main commands for performing substitutions in expressions. The **subs** command performs literal replacements. Multiple substitutions can be given in a set or a list.

```
> A := ( x^2 + y^2 ) / ( 3 * x + k ) ;
```

$$A := \frac{x^2 + y^2}{3x + k}$$

```
> subs( x = k , A ) ;
```

$$\frac{1}{4} \frac{k^2 + y^2}{k}$$

```
> subs( { x = k , y = k } , A ) ;
```

$$\frac{1}{2} k$$

```
> subs( [ x = c , y = c , k = c^2 - 3 * c ] , A ) ;
```

$$2$$

The **algsubs** command performs only one replacement, but it tries to rearrange expressions so that the substitution can be applied in more places. In the next example, **subs** finds a single instance of $1 + x^2$ and replaces it with k, so that the result contains both x and k. The **algsubs** command expresses the result in terms of k only.

```
> R := ( x^2 + 1 ) / ( x^6 + x^4 + 2 ) ;
```

$$R := \frac{x^2 + 1}{x^6 + x^4 + 2}$$

```
> subs( 1 + x^2 = k , R ) ;
```

$$\frac{k}{x^6 + x^4 + 2}$$

```
> algsubs( 1 + x^2 = k , R ) ;
```

$$\frac{k}{k^3 - 2k^2 + k + 2}$$

There is an automatic simplification, but no evaluation (see Section 2.13) after a substitution. Consequently, to insert a numerical value, it is best to use **eval**.

```
> H := sin( 1 - t ) / cos( 1 - t ) ;
```

$$H := -\frac{\sin(-1 + t)}{\cos(-1 + t)}$$

```
> subs( t = 1 , H ) ;   # No evaluation!
```

$$-\frac{\sin(0)}{\cos(0)}$$

```
> % ;   # Causes an evaluation
```

$$0$$

```
> eval( H , t = 1 ) ;   # Set t = 1 and evaluate
```

$$0$$

The **eval** command can also insert multiple values from a set or a list.

```
> B := cos( x ) + tan( y ) ;
```

$$B := \cos(x) + \tan(y)$$

```
> eval( B , [ x = Pi / 3 , y = Pi / 4 ] ) ;
```

$$\frac{3}{2}$$

3.4 Functions

Mathematical functions are represented by *functional operators* in Maple. These can be defined using arrow notation (- followed immediately by >).

```
> f := x -> 2 * x ;
```
$$f := x \rightarrow 2x$$

```
> f( 1 ) ;
```
$$2$$

```
> f( a + b ) ;
```
$$2a + 2b$$

It is important to understand the difference between operator definitions and ordinary assignments. This is illustrated by the following example.

```
> y := x^2 :
> x := 5 :
> y ;
```
$$25$$

```
> f := z -> z^2 ;
```
$$f := z \rightarrow z^2$$

```
> z := 5 :
> f ;
```
$$f$$

```
> f( 3 ) ;
```
$$9$$

Executing the first statement causes y to depend upon x, and the second assigns the value 5 to x. When the third statement is executed, y evaluates to x^2, and then x evaluates to 5, so that the result is 25. On the other hand, f is defined as an operator which takes one argument and returns the square of that argument as its result. The symbol z plays the role of a dummy variable, and assignments to z have no effect on f. The same operator could be defined using any other name in place of z.

```
> f := tomato -> tomato^2 ;
```

$$f := tomato \rightarrow tomato^2$$

```
> f( 3 ) ;
```

$$9$$

★ If Maple unexpectedly returns an expression unevaluated, check that all necessary operator definitions have been executed.

```
> g := x -> x^5 + 4 :
> restart :
> g( 2 ) ;  # restart deletes the definition of g
```

$$g(2)$$

★ If Maple returns an unexpected result, check that variables and arrows have not been omitted from operator definitions.

```
> h := x^2 :
> h( 2 ) ;  # h isn't a functional operator...
```

$$x(2)^2$$

Operators that depend on more than one variable can also be created using arrow notation. In this case, parentheses are needed around the variables before the arrow.

```
> g := ( x , y ) -> sin( x + y ) :
> g( 3.1 , 1.2 ) ;
```

$$-0.9161659367$$

Structures such as lists and sets can be used as arguments. The next example defines a functional operator that tests for proper subsets (i.e. $\subset$ as opposed to $\subseteq$; see Section 2.17).

```
> proper_subset := ( A , B )
                      -> evalb( A subset B and not A = B ) ;
```

$$proper\_subset := (A, B) \rightarrow evalb(A \subseteq B \textbf{ and not } A = B)$$

```
> proper_subset( { 1 } , { 1 , 2 } ) ;
```

$$true$$

```
> proper_subset( { a , b } , { a , b } ) ;
```

$$false$$

Functions with piecewise definitions can be created using `piecewise` along with the relational operators introduced in Section 2.15. In its basic form, `piecewise` takes pairs of arguments. The first argument in each pair describes a range and the second is a mathematical expression which is used on this range. For example, the function

$$f(x) = \begin{cases} -1 & \text{if } x \leq 0, \\ x^2 & \text{if } x > 0, \end{cases}$$

can be defined and used in Maple as follows.

```
> f := x -> piecewise( x <= 0 , -1 , x > 0 , x^2 ) ;
```
$$f := x \rightarrow piecewise(x \leq 0, -1, 0 < x, x^2)$$

```
> f( 1 / 2 ) ;
```
$$\frac{1}{4}$$

```
> f( -1 ) ;
```
$$-1$$

The boolean operators **and** and **or** can be used to set more than one condition or to apply a definition on more than one range.

```
> g := x -> piecewise( x >= -2 and x <= 2 , 0 ,
                                  x < -2 or x > 2 , x^2 ) :
> g( y ) ;
```
$$\begin{cases} 0 & -2 \leq y \text{ and } y \leq 2 \\ y^2 & y < -2 \text{ or } 2 < y \end{cases}$$

If an odd number of arguments is passed to piecewise, the last is interpreted as an 'elsewhere' or 'otherwise' clause, meaning it is used outside the ranges specified by the preceding arguments.

```
> g := x -> piecewise( x < -1 , x^2 , x > 1 , x , 1 ) :
> g( y ) ;
```
$$\begin{cases} y^2 & y < -1 \\ y & 1 < y \\ 1 & otherwise \end{cases}$$

To define a functional operator using the result of an earlier calculation, use the **unapply** command.

```
> expand( ( ( 1 + t )^3 - ( 1 + t + t^2 )^3 ) / t^2 ) ;
```

$$-t^4 - 3t^3 - 6t^2 - 6t - 3$$

```
> f := unapply( % , t ) ;
```

$$f := t \rightarrow -t^4 - 3t^3 - 6t^2 - 6t - 3$$

```
> f( 0 ) ;
```

$$-3$$

Multiple variables can be given separately, or in a list.

```
> A := expand( sin( x + y ) - sin( x - y ) ) ;
```

$$A := 2\cos(x)\sin(y)$$

```
> g := unapply( A , x , y ) ;
```

$$g := (x, y) \rightarrow 2\cos(x)\sin(y)$$

```
> g( Pi , Pi / 2 ) ;
```

$$-2$$

```
> h := unapply( A , [ x , y ] ) ;
```

$$h := (x, y) \rightarrow 2\cos(x)\sin(y)$$

```
> evalf( h( 0 , 1 ) ) ;
```

$$1.682941970$$

When an operator is defined using arrow notation, the expression to the right of the arrow undergoes a partial automatic simplification in which no approximate calculations are performed, and the meaning of ditto operators is not resolved (so something like **f := x -> %** will never work — use **unapply**). There is no evaluation on either side of the arrow. Therefore dummy variables are not affected by prior assignments. Similarly, a value assigned to a name is not affected if the same name is used as a dummy variable in an operator definition. In the next example, the fact that x has the value 4 has no effect when f is defined, and x still has the value 4 afterwards.

```
> x := 4 :   # Doesn't affect f
> f := x -> 2 * exp( x ) ;  # Doesn't affect x
```

$$f := x \rightarrow 2e^x$$

```
> f( 1 ) ;
```

$$2e$$

```
> x ;
```

$$4$$

Another consequence of the evaluation rules for arrow notation is that commands in an operator definition are not executed until the operator is used. In most circumstances this is the desired behaviour: Maple waits until values have been provided for dummy variables before attempting to apply the operation. However, a very common mistake is to expect Maple to perform some manipulations on the expression to the right of the arrow, as shown in the next example.

```
> g := x -> numer( ( x + 1 ) / ( x - 1 ) ) ;
```

$$g := x \rightarrow numer\left(\frac{x+1}{x-1}\right)$$

```
> g( 1 ) ;
Error, (in g) numeric exception: division by zero
```

Here, **numer** does not act until after the value 1 has been substituted for x, and the division has been attempted, leading to a disaster. To correctly define g using the result of the **numer** command, we should use **unapply**.

```
> g := unapply( numer( ( x + 1 ) / ( x - 1 ) ) , x ) ;
```

$$g := x \rightarrow x + 1$$

```
> g( 1 ) ;
```

$$2$$

The same technique can be used to replace parameters by their values before an operator is defined. In the next example, $f(x)$ and $g(x)$ depend on the parameter a. Arrow notation is used to apply the definition $f(x) = ax + 1$. Subsequently, when $f(4)$ is evaluated, a has the value 2, so the result returned is 9. When the value of a is changed to 0, this affects the definition of f, so that $f(4)$ now evaluates to 1. On the other hand, g is defined using the **unapply** command. Prior evaluation of the arguments causes a to be replaced by 2 before the definition is made. Hence, $g(x) = 2x + 1$, which does not change when a is set to 0.

```
> a := 2 :
> f := x -> a * x + 1 ;
```

$$f := x \rightarrow ax + 1$$

```
> g := unapply( a * x + 1 , x ) ;
```

$$g := x \rightarrow 2x + 1$$

```
> f(4) ;
```

$$9$$

```
> g(4) ;
```

$$9$$

```
> a := 0 :
> f( 4 ) ;
```

$$1$$

```
> g( 4 ) ;
```

$$9$$

Before moving on, it's worth mentioning that Maple's terminology with regard to functions is somewhat unusual. For example, in mathematics there is a tangent function, which is generally represented by the notation tan. However, in Maple the tangent function is implemented using a *procedure* (see Chapter 8 for more about these) called **tan**. The functional operators introduced in this section are all members of a special class of procedure. What Maple calls a *function* would usually be referred to as a *function call*, especially in computer science. Mathematically, an expression such as tan(1.2) is actually just a number, but when we enter this into Maple, we are instructing it to invoke its mechanism for computing tangents, hence the term function call.

```
> whattype( tan( 1.2 ) ) ;
```

$$float$$

```
> whattype( 'tan( 1.2 )' ) ;
```
function

```
> whattype( eval( tan ) ) ;
```
procedure

The need for **eval** in the last statement arises because procedures use last name evaluation. See Section 8.10 for more about the effect of applying **eval** to procedure names.

In this book, the term function is used in its usual mathematical sense. On the rare occasions when this is necessary, we will refer to function calls to avoid using the word function with two different meanings. We will use the term functional operator (or in some cases procedure) to refer to a Maple implementation of a mathematical function. The main thing to keep in mind to avoid any confusion is that the term functional operator refers to an object that most mathematicians would just think of as a function.

3.5 Limits

Limits can be computed using the **limit** command.

```
> limit( sin( x ) / x , x = 0 ) ;
```
1

The arguments undergo evaluation before Maple attempts to compute the limit itself, which can cause errors if the dummy variable has been used earlier in the worksheet.

```
> x := 5 :
> limit( x * exp( -x ) , x = infinity ) ;
Error, invalid input: limit expects its 2nd argument, p, to
be of type Or(name = algebraic, set(name = algebraic)), but
received 5 = infinity
```

As noted in Section 2.13, the unwanted prior evaluation can be prevented without the need to unassign x, or make any other changes, by using unevaluation quotes (in which case x will still have the value 5 after the limit is computed).

```
> x := 5 :
> limit( 'x * exp( -x )' , 'x' = infinity ) ;
```

$$0$$

```
> x ;
```

$$5$$

The *inert* form of the limit command, which begins with a capital letter, is useful for checking for prior assignments and other potential problems such as typographical errors. This places the operator 'on hold', but the rest of the expression still undergoes evaluation.

```
> a := -1 :
> Limit( arctan( a * t ) , t = infinity ) ;
```

$$\lim_{t \to \infty} (-\arctan(t))$$

Notice that the value for *a* has been substituted into the limit, and that Maple shows the lim operator in grey, to indicate that it is inert. Once it is clear that there are no problems with the input, the limit can be evaluated by changing the upper case L to lower case and executing again, or by using the **value** command.

```
> a := -1 :
> Q := Limit( arctan( a * t ) , t = infinity ) ;
```

$$Q := \lim_{t \to \infty} (-\arctan(t))$$

```
> value( Q ) ;
```

$$-\frac{1}{2}\pi$$

A similar effect can be achieved using unevaluation quotes, but this results in a temporary hold; the limit will be calculated after $n + 1$ evaluations, where *n* is the number of quote pairs.

```
> L := 'limit'( exp( t ) / cosh( t ) , t = infinity ) ;
```

$$L := \lim_{t \to \infty} \frac{e^t}{\cosh(t)}$$

```
> L ;
```

$$2$$

3.6 Summing Series

The **sum** command can be used to find the sum of a series.

```
> sum( 1 / j^2 , j = 1 .. infinity ) ;
```

$$\frac{1}{6}\pi^2$$

As with limits, there is an inert form which is useful for detecting problems with the input.

```
> Sum( j^2 , j = 1 .. m ) ;
```

$$\sum_{j=1}^{m} j^2$$

```
> value( % ) ;
```

$$\frac{1}{3}(m+1)^3 - \frac{1}{2}(m+1)^2 + \frac{1}{6}m + \frac{1}{6}$$

For finite series, the **sum** command may cause Maple to simply add the terms directly.

```
> sum( sin( j ) , j = 1 .. 8 ) ;
```

$$\sin(1) + \sin(2) + \sin(3) + \sin(4) + \sin(5) + \sin(6) + \sin(7) + \sin(8)$$

However, it will try summation by analytic methods if the number of terms is large (though of course this may not be possible).

```
> sum( sin( j ) , j = 1 .. 1000 ) ;
```

$$\frac{1}{2}\frac{\sin(1)\cos(1001)}{\cos(1)-1} - \frac{1}{2}\sin(1001) - \frac{1}{2}\frac{\sin(1)\cos(1)}{\cos(1)-1} + \frac{1}{2}\sin(1)$$

It is also possible to try certain methods used by the **sum** command individually (execute **?sum,details** for full details). The most useful command of this type (at least with simple series) is **Telescoping**. This is contained in the **DefiniteSum** package, which is a subpackage of **SumTools**. The term *telescoping* refers to the manner in which naval telescopes can be collapsed down toward their ends; one can see the motivation for this nomenclature by multiplying the geometric series

$$S_n = 1 + a + \cdots + a^n$$

by $(1-a)/(1-a)$ (assuming that $a \neq 1$).

```
> with( SumTools[ DefiniteSum ] ) :
> Telescoping( a^j , j = 1 .. 10 ) ;
```

$$\frac{a^{11}}{a-1} - \frac{a}{a-1}$$

```
> simplify( Telescoping( sin( j ) , j = 1 .. 8 ) ) ;
```

$$\frac{1}{2} \frac{\sin(1)\cos(9) - \sin(9)\cos(1) + \sin(9) - \sin(1)}{\cos(1) - 1}$$

Whilst **Telescoping** produces more concise results than **sum** in certain circumstances, it works with a narrower class of series, and fails in many cases.

```
> with( SumTools[ DefiniteSum ] ) :
> Telescoping( cos( j^2 ) , j = 1 .. 10000 ) ;
```

$$FAIL$$

By contrast, **sum** always evaluates finite series with known limits explicitly, though the result may not be useful unless **evalf** is applied.

```
> sum( cos( j^2 ) , j = 1 .. 10000 ) ;
                            # Generates a very large expression
> evalf( % ) ;
```

$$-7.818387626$$

Note that the order in which the terms in a series are summed can vary, leading to different rounding errors, and slightly different results. In cases where adding terms is known to be the best (or only) option, the **add** command is generally recommended, since it does not attempt summation by analytic means (see Section 2.20). In particular, **add**, and not **sum**, should be used to add together the elements of a container structure such as a list or set.

```
> add( 1 / j , j = 1 .. 10 ) ;
```

$$\frac{7381}{2520}$$

```
> L := [ 1 , 2 , 3 , 4 ] :
> add( L ) ;   # Maple 2015 & later
```

$$10$$

```
> add( L[j] , j = 1 .. 4 ) ;
```

$$10$$

If one of the limits of a sum is symbolic or infinite, **sum** may return the series unevaluated. Further evaluation may be possible later.

```
> s := sum( cos( j^2 ) , j = 1 .. m ) ;
```

$$s := \sum_{j=1}^{m} \cos(j^2)$$

```
> m := 3 :
> s ;
```

$$\cos(1) + \cos(4) + \cos(9)$$

Approximate values for infinite series can be obtained using **evalf**, even when exact evaluation is not possible.

```
> sum( exp( -j^2 ) / j , j = 1 .. infinity ) ;
```

$$\sum_{j=1}^{\infty} \frac{e^{-j^2}}{j}$$

```
> evalf( % ) ;
```

$$0.3770784254$$

★ Summing all terms in an infinite series is clearly impossible, so **add** cannot be used in such cases.

Applying **evalf** to the inert command **Sum** prevents Maple from attempting to sum an infinite series by analytic means, so that it uses approximate methods from the outset.

```
> evalf( Sum( exp( -j^2 ) / j , j = 1 .. infinity ) ) ;
```

$$0.3770784254$$

However, it usually doesn't take Maple very long to decide that summation by analytic means cannot be achieved, and there are some cases (typically involving slowly convergent series) where Maple's analytical methods work, but its approximate methods fail.

```
> evalf( Sum( sin( j ) / j , j = 1 .. infinity ) ) ;
```

$$\sum_{j=1}^{\infty} \frac{\sin(j)}{j}$$

```
> evalf( sum( sin( j ) / j , j = 1 .. infinity ) ) ;
```
$$1.070796327$$

For this reason, `evalf( sum( ... ) )` is preferable to the form with
Sum in most cases.

3.7 Differentiation

Expressions can be differentiated using `diff`.

```
> diff( x^2 + 1 , x ) ;
```
$$2x$$

The `diff` command can also be used to differentiate more than once.

```
> f := x -> x^4 :
> diff( f( x ) , x , x ) ;
```
$$12x^2$$

```
> diff( f( x ) , x , x , x ) ;
```
$$24x$$

The *sequence operator* `$` can be used to make repeated differentiations
more concise. For example, `x$3` and `y$2` evaluate to x, x, x and y, y,
respectively, and we can exploit this as follows.

```
> f := ( x , y ) -> cos( x^3 * y ) :
> diff( f( x , y ) , x$3 , y$2 ) ;
```
$$-27\sin(x^3y)x^{12}y^3 + 216\cos(x^3y)x^9y^2 + 384\sin(x^3y)x^6y$$
$$-120\cos(x^3y)x^3$$

There is an inert form of the differentiation command, `Diff`.

```
> f := ( x , y ) -> ( y^2 + x^2 ) * exp( x ) :
> Diff( f( x , y ) , x$5 , y$2 ) ;
```
$$\frac{\partial^7}{\partial y^2 \partial x^5}\left((y^2 + x^2)e^x\right)$$

```
> value( % ) ;
```
$$2e^x$$

Maple also has the *differential operator* D. The main difference between

D and `diff` is that the former differentiates operators, whereas the latter acts on expressions.

```
> D( arctan ) ;
```

$$z \to \frac{1}{z^2 + 1}$$

```
> diff( arctan( x ) , x ) ;
```

$$\frac{1}{x^2 + 1}$$

```
> D( arctan( x ) ) ;   # Wrong!
```

$$D(\arctan(x))$$

```
> diff( arctan , x ) ;   # Wrong!
```

$$0$$

The differentiation operator can be used to conveniently obtain the value of a derivative at a point.

```
> D( sin )( Pi ) ;
```

$$-1$$

Here, Maple differentiates the sine function and then passes the argument π to the resulting cosine function. The same result can be obtained using `diff` and `eval`.

```
> eval( diff( sin( x ) , x ) , x = Pi ) ;
```

$$-1$$

The short form with D is used in specifying boundary and initial conditions for differential equations (see Section 4.4). The D operator also provides a shortcut to avoid using **unapply** with derivatives.

```
> f := x -> x^2 :
> g := D( f ) ;
```

$$g := x \to 2x$$

To achieve the same effect using `diff` we need the following.

```
> f := x -> x^2 :
> g := unapply( diff( f( x ) , x ) , x ) ;
```

$$g := x \to 2x$$

3.8 Integration

To integrate an expression, use `int`.

```
> int( 2 * x , x ) ;
```

$$x^2$$

Note that this does not create a constant of integration. Definite integrals can be evaluated by providing a range for the integration variable.

```
> int( exp( -x ) , x = 0 .. 1 ) ;
```

$$1 - e^{-1}$$

```
> int( exp( -x^2 ) , x = -infinity .. infinity ) ;
```

$$\sqrt{\pi}$$

The inert integration command `Int` is particularly useful for checking that the input is correct. As usual, the operator can be activated using `value`.

```
> Int( ( 6 - cos( x )^2 + cos( x )^4 ) * tan( x )
                        / cos( x )^3 , x = 0 .. Pi / 4 ) ;
```

$$\int_0^{\frac{1}{4}\pi} \frac{(6 - \cos(x)^2 + \cos(x)^4)\tan(x)}{\cos(x)^3}\,\mathrm{d}x$$

```
> value( % ) ;
```

$$\frac{5}{2}\sqrt{2}$$

Maple is very good at evaluating integrals exactly, but in some cases it produces long expressions, or expressions that involve esoteric functions, both of which can be difficult for a human to interpret. To obtain a numerical result for a definite integral, use `evalf`.

```
> int( 1 / sqrt( 2 - sin( t )^2 ) , t = 0 .. 1 ) ;
```

$$\frac{1}{2}\sqrt{2}\,\mathrm{EllipticF}\left(\sin(1), \frac{1}{2}\sqrt{2}\right)$$

```
> evalf( % ) ;
```

$$0.7659499255$$

If `int` is unable to evaluate an integral, it will be returned unevaluated, but `evalf` still works.

```
> int( 1 / ( sin( x ) + x ) , x = 1 .. 2 ) ;
```

$$\int_1^2 \frac{1}{\sin(x) + x}\,\mathrm{d}x$$

```
> evalf( int( 1 / ( sin( x ) + x ) , x = 1 .. 2 ) ) ;
```

$$0.4140851550$$

Combining `evalf` with `int` in this way causes Maple to try analytic methods, and then resort to numerical approximations if these fail. On the other hand, using the inert form prevents exact evaluation of the integral, so that numerical approximations are used from the outset. In contrast to the case of series summation (Section 3.6), this is often much faster.

```
> evalf( Int( 1 / ( cos( x ) + x ) , x = 1 .. 2 ) ) ;
```

$$0.6378460922$$

★ Use `unapply` to define a functional operator using a previously calculated integral.

```
> int( 1 / sqrt( 1 - x^2 ) , x ) ;
```

$$\arcsin(x)$$

```
> f := unapply( % , x ) ;
```

$$f := x \rightarrow \arcsin(x)$$

```
> f( 1 ) ;
```

$$\frac{1}{2}\pi$$

Double and triple integrals can be entered as nested single integrals, or by specifying the integration variables and ranges in a list. In the following example, the inert form is used to check the input before the integrals are evaluated using `value`.

```
> Int( Int( x^2 , x = 0 .. y ) , y = 0 .. 1 ) ;
```

$$\int_0^1 \int_0^y x^2\,\mathrm{d}x\mathrm{d}y$$

```
> value( % ) ;
```

$$\frac{1}{12}$$

```
> Int( exp( -x^2 - y^2 ) ,
            [ x = 0 .. infinity , y = 0 .. infinity ] ) ;
```

$$\int_0^\infty \int_0^\infty e^{-x^2-y^2} \, \mathrm{d}x\mathrm{d}y$$

```
> value( % ) ;
```

$$\frac{1}{4}\pi$$

Apart from being slightly shorter, the form with a single integration command has the advantage that it enables Maple to use the limits in the outer integral to make assumptions when evaluating the inner integral. For example, consider the double integral

$$\int_1^2 \int_y^\infty \frac{1}{x^2} \, \mathrm{d}x\mathrm{d}y.$$

With the nested form, Maple will evaluate the inner integral without reference to the range for y (this is the effect of prior evaluation on the first argument to the outer **int** command). The fact that the inner integral does not exist if $y \le 0$ generates a warning. Using a single **int** with a list of variables and ranges avoids this.

```
> int( int( 1 / x^2 , x = y .. infinity ) , y = 1 .. 2 ) ;
Warning, unable to determine if 0 is between y and infinity;
try to use assumptions or use the AllSolutions option
```

$$\ln(2)$$

```
> int( 1 / x^2 , [ x = y .. infinity , y = 1 .. 2 ] ) ;
```

$$\ln(2)$$

There are also cases where assumptions on the outer variable cause the single **int** form to evaluate much more quickly.

★ The **VectorCalculus** package provides commands for surface, line and path integrals. Execute **?VectorCalculus,details** for more information.

3.9 Series Expansions

Series expansions can be obtained using the **series** command.

```
> series( cosh( x ) , x ) ;
```

$$1 + \frac{1}{2} x^2 + \frac{1}{24} x^4 + O(x^6)$$

```
> series( 1 / ( 1 - 2 * x ) , x ) ;
```

$$1 + 2x + 4x^2 + 8x^3 + 16x^4 + 32x^5 + O(x^6)$$

To remove the error term from a series expansion, use the **polynom** option for **convert**.

```
> convert( series( arctan( x ) , x ) , polynom ) ;
```

$$x - \frac{1}{3} x^3 + \frac{1}{5} x^5$$

It is also possible to perform a series expansion about an arbitrary point.

```
> series( log( x ) , x = 3 ) ;
```

$$\ln(3) + \frac{1}{3} (x - 3) - \frac{1}{18} (x - 3)^2 + \frac{1}{81} (x - 3)^3 - \frac{1}{324} (x - 3)^4$$

$$+ \frac{1}{1215} (x - 3)^5 + O((x - 3)^6)$$

The order at which terms are discarded from a series expansion is determined by the value of the **Order** environment variable, the default value of which is 6.

```
> series( exp( x ) , x ) ;
```

$$1 + x + \frac{1}{2} x^2 + \frac{1}{6} x^3 + \frac{1}{24} x^4 + \frac{1}{120} x^5 + O(x^6)$$

```
> Order := 8 :
> series( exp( x ) , x ) ;
```

$$1 + x + \frac{1}{2} x^2 + \frac{1}{6} x^3 + \frac{1}{24} x^4 + \frac{1}{120} x^5 + \frac{1}{720} x^6 + \frac{1}{5040} x^7 + O(x^8)$$

Alternatively, a third argument can be passed to the **series** command to obtain more (or fewer) terms.

```
> series( arccos( x ) , x , 11 ) ;
```

$$\frac{1}{2} \pi - x - \frac{1}{6} x^3 - \frac{3}{40} x^5 - \frac{5}{112} x^7 - \frac{35}{1152} x^9 + O(x^{11})$$

As with `Order`, the 11 here tells Maple to discard terms of order 11 or higher, not to retain terms up to x^{11}.

★ Maple will allow the assignment

> `Order := infinity :`

but this really isn't a good idea.

It should be noted that the order at which terms are discarded applies to intermediate calculations, and may be different from the leading order error in the answer. In the next example, Maple expands $e^x - 1$, retaining terms up to x^4, so that the error is $O(x^5)$. However, the result is subsequently divided by x, so ultimately the answer has an $O(x^4)$ error.

> `series( ( exp( x ) - 1 ) / x , x , 5 ) ;`

$$1 + \frac{1}{2}x + \frac{1}{6}x^2 + \frac{1}{24}x^3 + O(x^4)$$

In some cases, the error in the answer has a higher order than the error at intermediate steps.

> `series( sin( x ) * sinh( x ) , x , 5 ) ;`

$$x^2 + O(x^6)$$

Here, $\sin(x)$ and $\sinh(x)$ are expanded up to the terms in x^3. There are no terms in x^4, and the $O(x^5)$ terms are discarded. However, the leading term in both series is x, so the error goes from $O(x^5)$ to $O(x^6)$ when they are multiplied together. In some similar cases, Maple will underestimate the order of the error.

> `series( log( 1 + x ) * log( 1 - x ) , x , 5 ) ;`

$$-x^2 - \frac{5}{12}x^4 + O(x^5)$$

> `series( log( 1 + x ) * log( 1 - x ) , x , 8 ) ;`

$$-x^2 - \frac{5}{12}x^4 - \frac{47}{180}x^6 + O(x^8)$$

The second expansion clearly shows that the error in the first is $O(x^6)$. Interestingly, Maple remembers the outcome of series expansions, so if the order of the above statements is reversed, it uses the more accurate expansion to obtain the correct error when $O(x^5)$ terms are discarded.

```
> series( log( 1 + x ) * log( 1 - x ) , x , 8 ) ;
```

$$-x^2 - \frac{5}{12} x^4 - \frac{47}{180} x^6 + O(x^8)$$

```
> series( log( 1 + x ) * log( 1 - x ) , x , 5 ) ;
```

$$-x^2 - \frac{5}{12} x^4 + O(x^6)$$

In complicated cases, it is difficult to predict how many terms will be present in the final result on the basis of the number of terms used in intermediate calculations.

3.10 Assumptions

Some operations do not make sense unless assumptions are made about parameters involved. This is often the case for integration; for example, the integral

$$\int_0^\infty \frac{dx}{(x + a)^2(x + b)}$$

does not exist if $a \le 0$ or $b \le 0$. Attempting to evaluate such integrals using `int` will often produce unhelpful results such as 'undefined' or bizarre expressions involving arithmetic with infinity. To avoid this, assumptions can be specified at the end of a statement.

```
> Q := 1 / ( ( x + a )^2 * ( x + b ) ) :
> int( Q , x = 0 .. infinity ) assuming( a > 0 and b > 0 ) ;
```

$$-\frac{\ln(b)a - \ln(a)a + a - b}{a(a^2 - 2ab + b^2)}$$

Note the use of **and** here to apply multiple assumptions. Assumptions made using **assuming** are discarded after the statement to which they are attached has been executed. On the other hand, assumptions made using the **assume** command remain in force until the variable in question has been unassigned.

```
> assume( a > 0 ) :
> limit( exp( -a * t ) , t = infinity ) ;
```

$$0$$

```
> int( exp( -a * t ) , t = 0 .. infinity ) ;
```

$$\frac{1}{a\sim}$$

Here, Maple displays $a\sim$ to show that a is subject to an assumption. It is possible to prevent the tilde symbol from appearing, but doing so can produce misleading results, as demonstrated by the example at the end of this section. To enquire about assumptions on a variable, use the **about** command.

```
> assume( b :: integer ) ;
> about( b ) ;
Originally b, renamed b~:
  is assumed to be: integer
```

The **evalb** command introduced in Section 2.15 is not aware of assumptions. The **is** command can be used instead.

```
> assume( y > 0 ) ;
> evalb( y > 0 ) ;
```

$$0 < y\sim$$

```
> is( y > 0 ) ;
```

true

We conclude this section by examining the effect of assumptions in more detail. When the **assume** command is executed, a new variable is created with a tilde symbol ~ as the last character in its name, and this is assigned as the value of the original variable. The new variable is rather unusual. It is called an *escaped local variable* (see Section 8.3 for more about these), and access to this is only possible through its association with the original variable. It cannot be accessed using name quotes. Consider the following example.

```
> assume( n > 0 ) ;
> L := int( x^n , x = 0 .. 1 ) ;
```

$$L := \frac{1}{n\sim + 1}$$

```
> n := 1 ;
```

$$n := 1$$

```
> L ;
```

$$\frac{1}{n\sim + 1}$$

```
> `n~` := 1 ;
```

$$n\sim := 1$$

```
> L ;
```

$$\frac{1}{n\sim + 1}$$

Here, `assume( n > 0 )` creates an escaped local variable $n\sim$, and Maple assigns this as the value of n. After the second statement has been executed, the expression L includes a reference to the escaped local. The assignment $n := 1$ then breaks the association between n and $n\sim$, but it has no effect on L, because L does not contain a reference to n. The attempt to rectify the situation using name quotes in the penultimate statement fails, because this creates a new variable; it is not the same as the escaped local created by `assume`, despite the fact that it has the same name. The only way in which the escaped local $n\sim$ can now be accessed is through L itself (for example `denom( L ) - 1`). There are two ways around this horrible situation. One possibility is to substitute a value for n into L using `eval`.

```
> assume( n > 0 ) ;
> L := int( x^n , x = 0 .. 1 ) ;
```

$$L := \frac{1}{n\sim + 1}$$

```
> L := eval( L , n = 1 ) ;
```

$$L := \frac{1}{2}$$

When the last statement is executed, n evaluates to the escaped local $n\sim$ before being passed to `eval`. Using a slightly more elaborate construction, the escaped local can be replaced with n itself, thereby allowing us to continue working with L as an expression involving n.

```
> assume( n > 0 ) ;
> L := int( x^n , x = 0 .. 1 ) ;
```

$$L := \frac{1}{n\sim + 1}$$

```
> L := subs( n = 'n' , L ) ;
```

$$L := \frac{1}{n+1}$$

```
> unassign( 'n' ) ;
> L ;
```

$$\frac{1}{n+1}$$

Here, the left-hand n in the first argument to **subs** undergoes prior evaluation to the escaped local $n\sim$, but the unevaluation quotes block prior evaluation of the right-hand n. Hence **subs** now replaces $n\sim$ with n. The assumption on n must be removed by breaking its association with $n\sim$ using **unassign** before L is evaluated again, or else n will evaluate to the escaped local! The display of tilde symbols on variables with assumptions can be prevented by using the **interface** command to set **showassumed** to 0. This does not prevent the creation of escaped local variables, but these now have the same names as the original variables, which can be rather confusing.

```
> interface( showassumed = 0 ) :
> assume( a > 0 ) ;
> a ;
```

$$a$$

```
> b := a :
> a := 1 ;
```

$$a := 1$$

```
> b ;
```

$$a$$

Here, the **assume** command creates an escaped local variable called a, and the original a is assigned this as its value. When b is assigned the value a, the original a evaluates to the escaped local, but this doesn't happen on the left-hand side of the penultimate statement. Hence, when the final statement is reached, the original a has the value 1, but b evaluates to the escaped local a, which itself has no value. Clear?

4

Solving Equations

This chapter introduces three commands for solving equations: `solve`, which is used to solve one or more algebraic equations by exact methods, `fsolve`, which uses approximate methods, and `dsolve`, for solving differential equations. These share some important common properties.

- If no right-hand side is given, Maple will assume that this is zero.

  > `solve( x^2 + 4 * x + 3 ) ;`

  $$-1, -3$$

- Sometimes Maple won't return anything at all if it finds no solutions. There are two possible causes for this: there really are no solutions, or they do exist, but Maple is unable to find them.

  > `solve( exp( 1 / x ) = 0 ) ;   # No solutions exist`

- When solving multiple equations, it is usual to specify these in a set (see Section 2.17). Independent variables, and corresponding initial estimates or search ranges, can also be given in sets. In some cases lists can be used instead. To avoid undue complications, sets will be used throughout this chapter, except for one example in Section 4.3, where ordering of elements is crucial, and therefore sets cannot be used.

The `LinearSolve` command, which is used to solve linear systems of equations in matrix form, is considered in Section 5.7.

4.1 Solving Single Equations

Unsurprisingly, the basic command for solving equations is `solve`.

> `solve( 3 * x + 2 = 0 , x ) ;`

$$-\frac{2}{3}$$

Here, the second argument tells Maple to solve for the independent variable x. This can be omitted in simple cases (a drawback to doing so is discussed at the end of this section). However, in the next example, the second argument is needed to tell Maple to solve for y and not k.

```
> solve( exp( 3 * y ) - k = 0 , y ) ;
```

$$\frac{1}{3} \ln(k)$$

Note that y is not assigned the value $\ln(k)/3$ by the `solve` command (likewise x and $-2/3$ in the first example). To make the assignment, we can use `y := %` as the next statement, or solve and assign in a single step as follows.

```
> y := solve( exp( 3 * y ) - k = 0 , y ) ;
```

$$y := \frac{1}{3} \ln(k)$$

When `solve` finds more than one solution, it returns these as a sequence (see Section 2.16). An index in square brackets can be used to access the individual results, but in general it is a good idea to enclose the entire `solve` command in square brackets to create a list. This accounts for situations where a single solution is returned, which could otherwise cause problems in an automated worksheet.

```
> sols := solve( x^2 + 4 * x + 3 = 0 , x ) ;
```

$$sols := -1, -3$$

```
> sols[1] ;  # OK
```

$$-1$$

```
> sols[2] ;  # OK
```

$$-3$$

```
> sols := solve( 2 * y - 7 = 0 , y ) ;
```

$$sols := \frac{7}{2}$$

```
> sols[1] ;  # Disaster
```

$$\left(\frac{7}{2} \right)_1$$

```
> sols := [ solve( 2 * y - 7 = 0 , y ) ] ;   # Try again
```

$$sols := \begin{bmatrix} \dfrac{7}{2} \end{bmatrix}$$

```
> sols[1] ;
```

$$\frac{7}{2}$$

★ In conjunction with `mul` (see Section 2.20), the `solve` command can be used to form a factorisation of a polynomial with complex and/or radical roots without the need to provide a list of trial candidates (cf. `factor` in Section 3.1).

```
> p := x^4 + 4 * x^3 + 8 * x^2 + 12 * x + 15 :
> R := [ solve( p = 0 , x ) ] :
> mul( x - r , r in R ) ;
```

$$\left(x - I\sqrt{3}\right)\left(x + I\sqrt{3}\right)(x + 2 + I)(x + 2 - I)$$

Sometimes Maple won't give solutions explicitly.

```
> solve( x^4 - 3 * x^3 + 2 * x^2 + x + 1 = 0 , x ) ;
```

$RootOf(\_Z^4 - 3\_Z^3 + 2\_Z^2 + \_Z + 1, index = 1),$
$\quad RootOf(\_Z^4 - 3\_Z^3 + 2\_Z^2 + \_Z + 1, index = 2),$
$\quad RootOf(\_Z^4 - 3\_Z^3 + 2\_Z^2 + \_Z + 1, index = 3),$
$\quad RootOf(\_Z^4 - 3\_Z^3 + 2\_Z^2 + \_Z + 1, index = 4)$

The `explicit` option can be used to coerce it into displaying roots in terms of radicals wherever possible, but the result may be very long. Using `evalf` may produce more tractable results, but it should be noted that solving approximately with `fsolve` (see Section 4.3) is usually more efficient than solving exactly and then approximating the results.

```
> solve( x^4 - 3 * x^3 + x^2 + x + 1 = 0 , x ,
         explicit = true ) ;   # Produces a very long result.

> evalf( solve( x^4 - 3 * x^3 + x^2 + x + 1 = 0 , x ) ) ;
```

$1.389390683, 2.288794992, -0.3390928378 + 0.4466301000\,I,$
$\quad -0.3390928378 - 0.4466301000\,I$

Here, `explicit = true` can be abbreviated to just `explicit`, with the same effect.

★ Commands that accept an optional argument in the form '*key-word* = *value*', where *value* can be either `true` or `false`, often allow `= true` to be omitted. Apart from the `explicit` option to `solve` shown above, examples include the `discont` option for the `plot` command and the `filledregions` option for the `contourplot` command (see Chapter 6).

If the second argument to `solve` is omitted, Maple solves for all variables that remain in the first argument after it has undergone prior evaluation.

```
> solve( x + y = 0 ) ;  # Solve for both x and y
```
$$\{x = -y, y = y\}$$
```
> x := 2 :
> solve( x + y = 0 ) ;  # Solve for y (x evaluates to 2)
```
$$-2$$

In general, it is best to explicitly specify the variable(s) for which to solve, even when this is obvious. Failing to do so can lead to misleading results if an independent variable used in a `solve` command has been assigned a value earlier in the worksheet.

```
> x := 7 :
> solve( 4 * x + 3 = 0 ) ;  # Produces no output
```

No output is produced by the above example, because the left-hand side evaluates to 31 before the `solve` command is invoked, so no solutions are found. With the second argument included, Maple detects the problem.

```
> x := 7 ;
```
$$x := 7$$
```
> solve( 4 * x + 3 = 0 , x ) ;
Warning, solving for expressions other than names or
functions is not recommended.
Error, (in solve) a constant is invalid as a variable, 7
```

This issue can be avoided by using a new symbol as the independent variable, by unassigning *x* before invoking `solve` (see Section 2.11), or by using unevaluation quotes.

```
> x := 7 :
> solve( '4 * x + 3 = 0' , 'x' ) ;
```
$$-\frac{3}{4}$$

★ If an equation (or system of equations) is known to be linear, the
Linear command from the SolveTools package will obtain the
solution more rapidly than the generic solve command. Execute
?SolveTools,Linear for more details.

4.2 Solving Multiple Equations

The solve command can be used with simultaneous equations.

```
> eqn1 := x + y + z = 3 ;
```
$$eqn1 := x + y + z = 3$$

```
> eqn2 := 2 * x + 9 * y - 4 * z = 7 ;
```
$$eqn2 := 2x + 9y - 4z = 7$$

```
> eqn3 := 5 * x + 3 * y - z = 1 ;
```
$$eqn3 := 5x + 3y - z = 1$$

```
> solve( { eqn1 , eqn2 , eqn3 } , { x , y , z } ) ;
```
$$\left\{ x = -\frac{4}{9}, y = \frac{5}{3}, z = \frac{16}{9} \right\}$$

Remember that braces {} are used to create sets (see Section 2.17);
Maple solves a set of equations for a set of unknowns, and it returns a
set of equations as its result. A very useful command in this situation is
assign, which converts equations into assignments, making the solutions
available for use later.

```
> eqn1 := 3 * w * t = 1 :
> eqn2 := 5 * w * t^2 = 1 :
> solve( { eqn1 , eqn2 } , { w , t } ) ;
```
$$\left\{ t = \frac{3}{5}, w = \frac{5}{9} \right\}$$

```
> w ;
```
$$w$$

```
> assign( solve( { eqn1 , eqn2 } , { w , t } ) ) :
> w  ;
```

$$\frac{5}{9}$$

As with single equations, omitting the second argument to **solve** causes Maple to solve for all variables remaining in the first argument after any prior evaluations have been carried out. In the next example, q is assigned a value before **solve** is used, so Maple solves for x and y.

```
> q := 2 :
> eqn1 := x + y + q = 1 :
> eqn2 := x + 2 * y - q = 3 :
> solve( { eqn1 , eqn2 } ) ;
```

$$\{x = -7, y = 6\}$$

However, misleading results may be produced if an independent variable has been assigned a value earlier in the worksheet (as in the final paragraph of Section 4.1), so it is usually best to explicitly state the variables for which to solve.

Under some circumstances, the solutions to a system of equations are returned using **RootOf** notation with no index. In this case the **allvalues** command can be used to obtain all possible solutions. Alternatively, the **explicit** option for the **solve** command can be used.

```
> eqn1 := x^2 + y^2 = 1 :
> eqn2 := x - y = 2 :
> solve( { eqn1 , eqn2 } , { x , y } ) ;
```

$$\{x = RootOf\,(2\_Z^2 + 4\_Z + 3) + 2, y = RootOf\,(2\_Z^2 + 4\_Z + 3)\}$$

```
> allvalues( % ) ;
```

$$\left\{x = 1 + \frac{1}{2}\,I\sqrt{2}, y = -1 + \frac{1}{2}\,I\sqrt{2}\right\}, \left\{x = 1 - \frac{1}{2}\,I\sqrt{2}, y = -1 - \frac{1}{2}\,I\sqrt{2}\right\}$$

```
> solve( { eqn1 , eqn2 } , { x , y } , explicit ) ;
```

$$\left\{x = 1 + \frac{1}{2}\,I\sqrt{2}, y = -1 + \frac{1}{2}\,I\sqrt{2}\right\}, \left\{x = 1 - \frac{1}{2}\,I\sqrt{2}, y = -1 - \frac{1}{2}\,I\sqrt{2}\right\}$$

A particular set of solutions can be selected using an index in square brackets (cf. single equations with multiple solutions in Section 4.1). However, to account for situations in which only one solution is present,

it is best to enclose the entire `solve` command in square brackets, to
create a list.

```
> eq1  := x^2 + y^2 = 1 :
> eq2  := y = 2 * x :
> sols := [ solve( { eq1 , eq2 } , explicit ) ] ;
```

$$sols := \left[\left\{x = \frac{1}{5} \sqrt{5}, y = \frac{2}{5} \sqrt{5}\right\}, \left\{x = -\frac{1}{5} \sqrt{5}, y = -\frac{2}{5} \sqrt{5}\right\}\right]$$

```
> assign( sols[2] ) :
> x , y ;
```

$$-\frac{1}{5} \sqrt{5}, -\frac{2}{5} \sqrt{5}$$

4.3 Solving Approximately

Equations can be solved approximately using `fsolve`.

```
> fsolve( x^3 + x - sin( x ) + 2 = 0 , x ) ;
```

$$-1.200814175$$

As with `solve`, the second argument specifies the variable(s) for which
to solve. In general, `fsolve` tries to locate one solution to an equation
or system of equations. A single polynomial in a single variable is an
exception to this; in this case all the real roots are returned.

```
> fsolve( x^4 - 12 * x^3 + 10 * x^2 + 1 , x ) ;
```

$$1., 11.09822334$$

To obtain all complex solutions, use `fsolve` with the `complex` option.

```
> fsolve( x^4 - 12 * x^3 + 10 * x^2 + 1 , x , complex ) ;
```

$$-0.0491116676638473 - 0.296129289849573\,I,$$
$$-0.0491116676638473 + 0.296129289849573\,I, 1.,$$
$$11.0982233353277$$

Here Maple has switched to hardware arithmetic (see Section 2.8 for an
explanation) so that 15 significant figures are shown in the results.

The `fsolve` command accepts a search range or an initial estimate as
its second argument. These are useful if you already have some idea for
where to look for a root.

```
> f := x -> x * sin( x ) + 10 * x^3 - 20 * x^2 + 4 :
> evalf( f( -1 ) ) ;
```
$$-25.15852902$$

```
> evalf( f( 0 ) ) ;
```
$$4.$$

```
> # There must be a root between -1 and 0, so...
> fsolve( f( x ) , x = -1 .. 0 ) ;
```
$$-0.4153853154$$

```
> # Now look elsewhere...
> f( 1.8 ) ;
```
$$-0.72707426$$

```
> # Quite small; maybe there is a root nearby.
> fsolve( f( x ) , x = 1.8 ) ;
```
$$1.827263041$$

A system of equations or expressions contained in a set can be used as the first argument to **fsolve**. The variables for which to solve can also be given in a set.

```
> eqn1 := x^2 - y^3 + z = 0 :
> eqn2 := sin( x ) + exp( -y ) - z^2 = 0 :
> eqn3 := cos( x ) - z = 0 :
> fsolve( { eqn1 , eqn2 , eqn3 } , { x , y , z } ) ;
```
$$\{x = -10.08561146, y = 4.655934577, z = -0.7894809220\}$$

Similarly, a set of ranges or initial guesses can be provided when solving simultaneous equations.

```
> eq1 := x^2 + y^2 = 1 :
> eq2 := y = x^3 :
> fsolve( { eq1 , eq2 } , { x = 0 .. 1 , y = 0 .. 1 } ) ;
```
$$\{x = 0.8260313577, y = 0.5636241622\}$$

```
> fsolve( { eq1 , eq2 } , { x = -0.8 , y = -0.5 } ) ;
```
$$\{x = -0.8260313577, y = -0.5636241622\}$$

The **fsolve** command can accept a functional operator (more generally, a procedure) as its first argument, in which case it looks for an argument which causes this to evaluate to zero.

```
> g := x -> cos( x ) - x :
> fsolve( g ) ;
```

$$0.7390851332$$

As before, an initial estimate for the root or a search range can be provided as a second argument.

```
> y := x -> 4 * x * cos( x ) -  x^3 + 1 :
> fsolve( y , -1 ) ;  # N.B. no x = before -1
```

$$-1.036025382$$

```
> fsolve( y , 1 .. 2 ) ;  # N.B. no x = before 1 .. 2
```

$$1.321111087$$

More than one functional operator can be provided as the first argument to fsolve in a set or list, but in this case search ranges and initial estimates must be contained in lists, because the ordering of the entries is used to determine which range or estimate is to be used for which variable. The next example finds two solutions to the equations

$$(x - 1)^2 + 4y^2 = 4 \quad \text{and} \quad (x - 2)^2 + (y - 2)^2 = 9,$$

using fsolve. The operators f and g are defined to represent the differences between the left- and right-hand sides, so that they evaluate to zero at the points where solutions occur.

```
> f := ( x , y ) -> ( x - 1 )^2 + 4 * y^2 - 4 ;
```

$$f := (x, y) \rightarrow (x - 1)^2 + 4y^2 - 4$$

```
> g := ( x , y ) -> ( x - 2 )^2 + ( y - 2 )^2 - 9 ;
```

$$g := (x, y) \rightarrow (x - 2)^2 + (y - 2)^2 - 9$$

```
> fsolve( [ f , g ] , [ 1 , -1 ] ) ;  # Use initial guesses
```

$$[1.5343725608635682, -0.96364489909355512]$$

```
> fsolve( [ f , g ] , [ -1 .. 0 , 0 .. 1 ] ) ;  # Use ranges
```

$$[-0.63894206052515499, 0.57312060734228515]$$

Note that Maple has switched to hardware arithmetic, and provided answers to 15 significant figures (see Section 2.8).

If the second argument to fsolve is omitted, Maple will solve for

all variables remaining in the first argument after prior evaluations have
been carried out.

```
> r := 2 :
> fsolve( x^3 - r = 0 ) ;   # Automatically solves for x
```
$$1.259921050$$
```
> f := ( x , y ) -> ( x - 1 )^3 + 4 * y^2 - 4 ;
```
$$f := (x, y) \rightarrow (x - 1)^3 + 4y^2 - 4$$
```
> y := 0.1 :
> fsolve( f( x , y ) = 0 ) ;   # Automatically solves for x
```
$$2.582091979$$

In fact the second argument usually can be omitted if no initial estimate
or search range is to be specified, because (unlike solving exactly) solving
for all variables is invariably the desired behaviour. Indeed, attempting
to numerically solve an equation involving fixed symbolic parameters
does not make sense, and leads to an error.

```
> fsolve( x^2 + k * x - 3 = 0 , x ) ;
Error, (in fsolve) k is in the equation, and is not
solved for
```

As the next example demonstrates, specifying the variable(s) for which to
solve helps to detect problems caused by assignments made earlier in the
worksheet, as it does when solving exactly (Section 4.1), but the usual
remedy using unevaluation quotes doesn't always work with `fsolve`.

```
> x := 0 :
> fsolve( x^3 - exp( x ) - 1 = 0 ) ;   # Produces no output

> fsolve( x^3 - exp( x ) - 1 = 0 , x ) ;
Error, (in fsolve) invalid arguments
> fsolve( 'x^3 - exp( x ) - 1 = 0' , 'x' ) ;
Error, (in fsolve) invalid arguments
```

Here, x evaluates to 0 before being passed to `fsolve`, so that no solutions
are found at the first attempt. In the second attempt, prior evaluation of the
second argument results in Maple being told to use 0 as the independent
variable, causing an error, which is preferable to a misleading lack of
results. In the last statement, prior evaluation is blocked, but an error

occurs because *x* undergoes evaluation at some time *after* being passed to `fsolve`, which is rather unusual behaviour for a Maple command. The best way to avoid this is to use functional operators (or more generally, procedures), rather than equations or expressions.

```
> x := 0 :
> g := x -> x^3 - exp( x ) - 1 :
> fsolve( g ) ;   # But not fsolve( g( x ) ) ;
```

$$2.081116467$$

```
> fsolve( g , 4 .. 5 ) ;   # Use a search range
```

$$4.503671127$$

4.4 Differential Equations

The `dsolve` command is used to solve ordinary differential equations (ODEs).

```
> diff( y( x ) , x ) + A * y( x ) = 0 ;
```

$$\frac{d}{dx}y(x) + Ay(x) = 0$$

```
> dsolve( % , y( x ) ) ;
```

$$y(x) = \_C1e^{-Ax}$$

Maple uses the notation $\_C1, \_C2, \dots$ to represent arbitrary constants in the solution. The second argument to `dsolve` tells Maple what function it should solve for. This can be omitted in most cases. Provided that the first argument contains derivatives of only one function there can be no ambiguity, and Maple will work out what to do automatically.

```
> dsolve( x * diff( y( x ) , x ) + y( x ) = x ) ;
```

$$y(x) = \frac{1}{2}x + \frac{\_C1}{x}$$

However, it can't do this if the first argument to `dsolve` contains derivatives of more than one function.

```
> dsolve( diff( y( x ) , x , x )
                  = diff( z( x ) , x ) , y( x ) ) ;
```

$$y(x) = \int z(x)dx + \_C1x + \_C2$$

```
> dsolve( diff( y( x ) , x , x )
                    = diff( z( x ) , x ) , z( x ) ) ;
```

$$z(x) = \frac{d}{dx} y(x) + \_C1$$

```
> dsolve( diff( y( x ) , x , x ) = diff( z( x ) , x ) ) ;
Error, (in dsolve) Required a specification of the
indeterminate function
```

Boundary and initial conditions can also be given; here one must use D to denote differentiation, as described in Section 3.7. In the next example, the first ODE is solved subject to the boundary conditions $y(0) = 0$ and $y(1) = 1$, and the second is solved subject to the initial conditions $z(0) = 0$ and $z'(0) = 1$.

```
> ode1 := diff( y( x ) , x , x ) + diff( y( x ) , x )
                                    - 2 * y( x ) = 0 ;
```

$$ode1 := \frac{d^2}{dx^2}y(x) + \frac{d}{dx}y(x) - 2y(x) = 0$$

```
> dsolve( { ode1 , y( 0 ) = 0 , y( 1 ) = 1 } ) ;
```

$$y(x) = -\frac{e^x}{e^{-2} - e} + \frac{e^{-2x}}{e^{-2} - e}$$

```
> ode2 := diff( z( t ) , t , t ) + z( t ) = 0 ;
```

$$ode2 := \frac{d^2}{dt^2}z(t) + z(t) = 0$$

```
> dsolve( { ode2 , z( 0 ) = 0 , D( z )( 0 ) = 1 } ) ;
```

$$z(t) = \sin(t)$$

Note that the ODE and boundary or initial conditions are enclosed in braces, to create a set. Defining a functional operator using the solution to a differential equation requires some contortions. It is tempting to think that **assign** might be useful here, but it is not so: in the last example, this would convert $z(t) = \sin(t)$ into $z(t) := \sin(t)$, which is not what we require. Instead, use **rhs** to extract the right-hand side and then use **unapply**.

```
> ode := diff( z( t ) , t , t ) + z( t ) = 0 :
> dsolve( { ode , z( 0 ) = 0 , D( z )( 0 ) = 1 } ) ;
```

$$z(t) = \sin(t)$$

```
> z := unapply( rhs( % ) , t ) ;
```

$$z := t \to \sin(t)$$

```
> z( Pi ) ;
```

$$0$$

Coupled systems can also be solved using `dsolve`. In this case, Maple solves a set of equations and conditions for a set of unknown functions.

```
> eqn1 := diff( A( t ) , t ) = A( t ) + 4 * B( t ) ;
```

$$eqn1 := \frac{d}{dt} A(t) = A(t) + 4B(t)$$

```
> eqn2 := diff( B( t ) , t ) = A( t ) - 2 * B( t ) ;
```

$$eqn2 := \frac{d}{dt} B(t) = A(t) - 2B(t)$$

```
> ics := A( 0 ) = 0 , B( 0 ) = 1 ;
```

$$ics := A(0) = 0, \; B(0) = 1$$

```
> dsolve( { eqn1 , eqn2 , ics } , { A( t ) , B( t ) } ) ;
```

$$\left\{ A(t) = \frac{4}{5} e^{2t} - \frac{4}{5} e^{-3t}, \; B(t) = \frac{1}{5} e^{2t} + \frac{4}{5} e^{-3t} \right\}$$

There are many differential equations that cannot be solved exactly in terms of known functions. One possibility for this situation is a series solution.

```
> ode := diff( y( x ) , x , x ) + x^3 * diff( y( x ) , x )
                                        + x * y(x) = 0 ;
```

$$ode := \frac{d^2}{dx^2} y(x) + x^3 \left(\frac{d}{dx} y(x) \right) + xy(x) = 0$$

```
> bcs := y( 0 ) = 0 , D( y )( 0 ) = 2 :
> dsolve( { ode , bcs } , y( x ) , series ) ;
```

$$y(x) = 2x - \frac{1}{6} x^4 - \frac{1}{10} x^5 + O(x^6)$$

To obtain further terms, it is necessary to increase the value of the **Order** environment variable (see Section 3.9). When the **series** option is used, the second argument to `dsolve` (the function for which to solve) cannot be omitted. To calculate a solution using a numerical method, use the `numeric` option. The `dsolve` command then generates a procedure which can be used to obtain the solution given a value for the independent variable. The second argument to `dsolve` is mandatory in this case as well.

```
> ode := diff( y( x ) , x ) = x + ( x + y( x ) )^4 ;
```
$$ode := \frac{\mathrm{d}}{\mathrm{d}x} y(x) = x + (x + y(x))^4$$

```
> sol := dsolve( { ode , y(0) = 1 } , y( x ) , numeric ) ;
```
$$sol := \mathbf{proc}(x\_rkf45) \ldots \mathbf{end\ proc}$$

```
> sol( 0.1 ) ;
```
$$[x = 0.1, y(x) = 1.16673184290376]$$

```
> sol( 0.2 ) ;
```
$$[x = 0.2, y(x) = 1.81574294037041]$$

Here, Maple has switched to hardware arithmetic (see Section 2.8) and computed results to 15 significant figures.

Differential equations make up a huge part of applied mathematics, and as such a full treatment of all the facilities provided by Maple is far beyond the scope of this book. More information about the options available for use with `dsolve` can be obtained using `?dsolve` and `?dsolve,details`. Maple can also solve partial differential equations; for more information see `?pdsolve` and `?PDEtools`.

5

Linear Algebra

This allegedly shallow and outdated mode of thinking has now been superseded, according to the postmodernists, by a much deeper "nonlinear thought". The precise content of this new mode of thought is never explained very clearly — that would, perhaps, be too linear...

Alan Sokal, 'Beyond the Hoax'[1]

Mechanisms for creating matrices and vectors are available by default in Maple. Basic operations such as matrix addition and multiplication are also available. However, to access the full range of linear algebra facilities, it is necessary to load the `LinearAlgebra` package.

```
> with( LinearAlgebra ) :
```

This (along with the `VectorCalculus` package) supersedes the older `linalg` package, which should not be used in new worksheets. Also deprecated are the `vector` and `matrix` commands (with lower case `v` and `m`). Use `Vector` and `Matrix` instead.

★ To save time entering long commands and package names, type the first few letters, and then press ⌐escape⌐ to bring up a list of possible completions.

5.1 Creating Matrices and Vectors

There are several ways to create a matrix or a vector. If the entries are to be typed manually, the most concise method is to use *angle brackets* <>. A sequence of entries inside angle brackets produces a column vector, whereas using vertical bars | in place of commas generates a row vector.

---

[1] Oxford University Press (www.oup.com), 2008. Reprinted with permission.

117

> < a , b , c > ;

$$\begin{bmatrix} a \\ b \\ c \end{bmatrix}$$

> < a | b | c > ;

$$[a \; b \; c]$$

For a matrix, each sequence of entries can represent either a row or a column. In the former case, the sequences (not the entries!) must be separated by semicolons, and in the latter by vertical bars.

> < 1 , 2 , 3 ; 4 , 5 , 6 ; 7 , 8 , 9 > ;

$$\begin{bmatrix} 1 & 2 & 3 \\ 4 & 5 & 6 \\ 7 & 8 & 9 \end{bmatrix}$$

> < 1 , 2 | 4 , 5 | 6 , 8 > ;

$$\begin{bmatrix} 1 & 4 & 6 \\ 2 & 5 & 8 \end{bmatrix}$$

A number of more elaborate constructions are possible using angle brackets; execute **?MVshortcut** for full details. Zero vectors and zero matrices can be constructed using the **Vector** and **Matrix** commands. The **fill** option can be used to initialise a vector or matrix filled with something other than zeros.

> Vector(2) ;

$$\begin{bmatrix} 0 \\ 0 \end{bmatrix}$$

> Vector[row](3 , fill = 1) ;

$$[1 \; 1 \; 1]$$

> Matrix(2 , 3) ;

$$\begin{bmatrix} 0 & 0 & 0 \\ 0 & 0 & 0 \end{bmatrix}$$

> Matrix(2 , fill = Pi) ;

$$\begin{bmatrix} \pi & \pi \\ \pi & \pi \end{bmatrix}$$

In the last statement, the number of columns is omitted. Maple assumes that this is equal to the number of rows, so a square matrix is created.

Lists can be converted into vectors, using the **Vector** command, or the **convert** command.

```
> U := Vector( [ 5 , -1 ] ) :
> V := Vector[ row ]( [ f , g ] ) :
> U , V ;
```

$$\begin{bmatrix} 5 \\ -1 \end{bmatrix}, [f \ g]$$

```
> U := convert( [ 1 , Pi , q ] , Vector ) :
> V := convert( [ 1 , 2 , 3 ] , Vector[ row ] ) :
> U , V ;
```

$$\begin{bmatrix} 1 \\ \pi \\ q \end{bmatrix}, [1 \ 2 \ 3]$$

There is no command analogous to **Vector** for conversion back into a list, but **convert(V , list)** is permitted for any vector V. A matrix can be generated from a list of lists, in which each inner list contains the entries for one row.

```
> A := convert( [ [ 1 , 2 ] , [ 4 , 0 ] ] , Matrix ) :
> M := Matrix( [ [ a , b ] , [ 0 , Pi ] ] ) :
> A , M ;
```

$$\begin{bmatrix} 1 & 2 \\ 4 & 0 \end{bmatrix}, \begin{bmatrix} a & b \\ 0 & \pi \end{bmatrix}$$

Yet another possibility is to use a functional operator (more generally, a procedure) to initialise each element of a vector or matrix. This is useful in cases where the entries follow a simple pattern.

```
> f := j -> j^2 :
> Vector( 3 , f ) ;
```

$$\begin{bmatrix} 1 \\ 4 \\ 9 \end{bmatrix}$$

```
> Vector[ row ]( 4 , j -> y^(j-1) ) ;
```

$$[1 \ y \ y^2 \ y^3]$$

```
> f := ( j , p ) -> j^2 + p - 2 :
> Matrix( 3 , 4 , f ) ;
```

$$\begin{bmatrix} 0 & 1 & 2 & 3 \\ 3 & 4 & 5 & 6 \\ 8 & 9 & 10 & 11 \end{bmatrix}$$

```
> g := ( j , p ) -> I^j * x^p :
> Matrix( 4 , g ) ;
```

$$\begin{bmatrix} Ix & Ix^2 & Ix^3 & Ix^4 \\ -x & -x^2 & -x^3 & -x^4 \\ -Ix & -Ix^2 & -Ix^3 & -Ix^4 \\ x & x^2 & x^3 & x^4 \end{bmatrix}$$

Execute ?Matrix and ?Vector for more details about the options for constructing matrices and vectors.

5.2 Accessing Vector and Matrix Entries

The individual entries in a vector can be accessed using an index in square brackets. Assignments to the entries can be made in the usual way.

```
> V := Vector( 3 ) ;
```

$$V := \begin{bmatrix} 0 \\ 0 \\ 0 \end{bmatrix}$$

```
> V[1] ;
```

$$0$$

```
> V[2] := 4 :
> V ;
```

$$\begin{bmatrix} 0 \\ 4 \\ 0 \end{bmatrix}$$

To access the elements of a matrix, a row number and a column number must be given, separated by a comma.

```
> A := Matrix( 2 , 2 , fill = a ) :
> A[1,2] := 7 :
> A ;
```

$$\begin{bmatrix} a & 7 \\ a & a \end{bmatrix}$$

Parentheses can also be used to access vector and matrix elements, but $V(4)$ could be mistaken for a function call, whereas $V[4]$ cannot, so this is not generally recommended. However, there is one effect that can only be achieved using parentheses: making an assignment to an entry that is out of range automatically causes the vector or matrix to expand, whereas it causes an error if square brackets are used.

```
> M := Matrix( 2 , 2 , fill = 1 ) ;
```

$$M := \begin{bmatrix} 1 & 1 \\ 1 & 1 \end{bmatrix}$$

```
> M[3,3] := 5 ;
Error, Matrix index out of range
> M(3,3) := 5 ;
```

$$\begin{bmatrix} 1 & 1 & 0 \\ 1 & 1 & 0 \\ 0 & 0 & 5 \end{bmatrix}$$

Ranges can be used to access multiple elements of a matrix or vector simultaneously, exactly as described in Section 2.18. In the next example, the value π is placed in every entry in the first row of the matrix A.

```
> A := Matrix( 3 , 3 ) :
> A[1,..] := Pi :
> A ;
```

$$\begin{bmatrix} \pi & \pi & \pi \\ 0 & 0 & 0 \\ 0 & 0 & 0 \end{bmatrix}$$

Thus, a scalar assignment to a matrix, vector or part thereof causes the value on the right-hand side to appear in every specified entry on the left-hand side. It is also possible to overwrite sections of a matrix or vector with part or all of another matrix or vector.

```
> A := Matrix( 3 , 3 ) :
> V := < a , b > :
> A[1,2..3] := V :
> A[2..3,1] := V :
> A ;
```

$$\begin{bmatrix} 0 & a & b \\ a & 0 & 0 \\ b & 0 & 0 \end{bmatrix}$$

Here, the vector V is copied into the top right and the bottom left of the matrix A. In each case, two entries in A are overwritten by the two components of V. Overwriting multiple entries in a vector or matrix with a list has a different effect: the whole list will be copied into each specified position.

```
> v        := Vector( 4 ) :
> v[1..3] := [ a , b , c ] :
> v ;
```

$$\begin{bmatrix} [a, b, c] \\ [a, b, c] \\ [a, b, c] \\ 0 \end{bmatrix}$$

To avoid this, convert the list into a matrix or vector before making the assignment.

```
> v        := Vector( 4 ) :
> v[1..3] := Vector( [ a , b , c ] ) :
> v ;
```

$$\begin{bmatrix} a \\ b \\ c \\ 0 \end{bmatrix}$$

5.3 Displaying Matrices and Vectors

Maple won't display a matrix or vector whose size in any dimension is greater than the **rtablesize** interface variable, the default value of which is 10. This can be changed using the **interface** command.

```
> B := Matrix( 2 , 11 ) ;
```

$$B := \begin{bmatrix} 2 \times 11 \ Matrix \\ Data \ Type: \ anything \\ Storage: \ rectangular \\ Order: \ Fortran\_order \end{bmatrix}$$

```
> interface( rtablesize = 20 ) :
> B ;
```

$$\begin{bmatrix} 0 & 0 & 0 & 0 & 0 & 0 & 0 & 0 & 0 & 0 & 0 \\ 0 & 0 & 0 & 0 & 0 & 0 & 0 & 0 & 0 & 0 & 0 \end{bmatrix}$$

★ Setting `rtablesize` to `infinity` allows Maple to display all matrices and vectors.

5.4 Addition, Multiplication and Scalar Products

Basic calculations involving matrices and vectors, such as addition and subtraction can be performed using ordinary arithmetic operators; there is no need to include a tilde symbol to request an element-wise operation (see Section 2.19).

```
> A := < a , b ; c , d > ;
```

$$A := \begin{bmatrix} a & b \\ c & d \end{bmatrix}$$

```
> B := < -a , c ; c , 0 > ;
```

$$B := \begin{bmatrix} -a & c \\ c & 0 \end{bmatrix}$$

```
> A + B ;
```

$$\begin{bmatrix} 0 & b+c \\ 2c & d \end{bmatrix}$$

```
> 2 * A ;
```

$$\begin{bmatrix} 2a & 2b \\ 2c & 2d \end{bmatrix}$$

```
> u := < 1 , 2 > :
> v := < 3 , 4 > :
```

```
> u - 2 * v ;
```

$$\begin{bmatrix} -5 \\ -6 \end{bmatrix}$$

Matrix multiplication is indicated using a dot . rather than an asterisk.

```
> A := < 1 , 2 ; 4 , 0 > ;
```

$$A := \begin{bmatrix} 1 & 2 \\ 4 & 0 \end{bmatrix}$$

```
> B := < 2 , 3 ; -1 , 4 > ;
```

$$B := \begin{bmatrix} 2 & 3 \\ -1 & 4 \end{bmatrix}$$

```
> v := < 5 , -1 > ;
```

$$v := \begin{bmatrix} 5 \\ -1 \end{bmatrix}$$

```
> A . v ;
```

$$\begin{bmatrix} 3 \\ 20 \end{bmatrix}$$

```
> A . B , B . A ;
```

$$\begin{bmatrix} 0 & 11 \\ 8 & 12 \end{bmatrix}, \begin{bmatrix} 14 & 4 \\ 15 & -2 \end{bmatrix}$$

The general rule is that asterisks denote commutative multiplication (where $x * y = y * x$) whereas a dot indicates a multiplication that is not commutative. Scalar products can also be calculated using the . operator. In general (allowing for complex vector elements), scalar products are not commutative, due to conjugation of the left operand.

```
> c := < 1 , 2 > :
> d := < 2 , 1 + I > :
> c . d ;
```

$$4 + 2I$$

```
> d . c ;
```

$$4 - 2I$$

It should be noted that the noncommutative multiplication operator . has the same level of precedence as the commutative operator * (see

Section 2.3). This sets a trap for the unwary. Consider the following example, involving a complex exponential and a scalar product (a type of expression that appears frequently in wave theory).

```
> k := < Pi , 0 > ;
```

$$k := \begin{bmatrix} \pi \\ 0 \end{bmatrix}$$

```
> r := < 1 / 2 , 1 > ;
```

$$r := \begin{bmatrix} \frac{1}{2} \\ 1 \end{bmatrix}$$

```
> exp( I * k . r ) ;
```

$$-I$$

Most human mathematicians would read the expression $e^{ik \cdot r}$ as $e^{i(k \cdot r)}$, and since $\mathbf{k} \cdot \mathbf{r} = \pi/2$ here, we might expect Maple to produce the result I. However, * and . have equal precedence, so by working from left to right, Maple obtains a scalar product in which the left operand is complex, and conjugation then causes the appearance of the unexpected minus sign. One way to avoid this is to use the **DotProduct** command from the **LinearAlgebra** package, but some might consider the necessary typing excessive and prefer to simply use parentheses.

```
> with( LinearAlgebra ) :
> k := < Pi , 0 > :
> r := < 1 / 2 , 1 > :
> exp( I * DotProduct( k , r ) ) ;
```

$$I$$

```
> exp( I * ( k . r ) ) ;
```

$$I$$

5.5 Vector Products and Norms

Vector products can be computed using the **CrossProduct** command, or the **&x** operator, both of which are part of the **LinearAlgebra** package.

```
> with( LinearAlgebra ) :
> b := < 1 , 2 , -1 > :
> c := < 3 , 1 ,  0 > :

> CrossProduct( b , c ) ;
```

$$\begin{bmatrix} 1 \\ -3 \\ -5 \end{bmatrix}$$

```
> c &x b ;
```

$$\begin{bmatrix} -1 \\ 3 \\ 5 \end{bmatrix}$$

The &x operator has higher precedence than the noncommutative multiplication operator. The next example works because the vector product is evaluated before the scalar product (the opposite order would lead to an error because $a \cdot b$ returns a scalar result, which cannot be used as an operand in a vector product).

```
> a := < 4 , 3 ,  1 > :
> b := < 1 , 2 , -1 > :
> c := < 3 , 1 ,  0 > :
> a . b &x c ;
```

$$-10$$

To calculate the length of a vector, use the Norm command.

```
> with( LinearAlgebra ) :
> b := < 3 , 4 > :
> Norm( b , 2 ) ;
```

$$5$$

In general, if **b** has elements $b_1, \ldots, b_n$, then Norm(b , p) returns the value

$$\|\mathbf{b}\|_p = (|b_1|^p + |b_2|^p + \cdots + |b_n|^p)^{1/p}.$$

Thus, $p = 2$ produces the Euclidean norm

$$\|\mathbf{b}\|_2 = \sqrt{|b_1|^2 + |b_2|^2 + \cdots + |b_n|^2}.$$

The Norm command can be used without a second argument, but the value it then chooses for p depends on which packages have been loaded, and in which order. The **LinearAlgebra** package defaults to the infinity norm (the largest of the magnitudes $|b_1|, \ldots, |b_n|$), whereas the **VectorCalculus** package uses the Euclidean norm.

```
> b := < 1 , 2 , -1 > :
> with( LinearAlgebra ) :
> Norm( b ) ;
```

$$2$$

```
> with( VectorCalculus ) :
> Norm( b ) ;
```

$$\sqrt{6}$$

★ Never use **Norm** without a second argument.

5.6 Other Matrix Operations

Many commands that operate on matrices have self-explanatory purposes.

```
> with( LinearAlgebra ) :
> A := < 1 , 2 ; 0 , -4 > ;
```

$$A := \begin{bmatrix} 1 & 2 \\ 0 & -4 \end{bmatrix}$$

```
> Transpose( A ) ;
```

$$\begin{bmatrix} 1 & 0 \\ 2 & -4 \end{bmatrix}$$

```
> MatrixInverse( A ) ;
```

$$\begin{bmatrix} 1 & \dfrac{1}{2} \\ 0 & -\dfrac{1}{4} \end{bmatrix}$$

```
> Determinant( A ) ;
```

$$-4$$

```
> Eigenvalues( A ) ;
```

$$\begin{bmatrix} 1 \\ -4 \end{bmatrix}$$

Computing the exact eigenvalues of a 3×3 or larger matrix may result in a long and complicated expression. As usual, `evalf` can be applied to produce an approximate result. Note that the `Eigenvalues` command returns a vector containing the eigenvalues, though a list would perhaps be a more logical structure to use. Similarly, the `Eigenvectors` command returns a vector containing the eigenvalues, followed by a matrix in which each column is an eigenvector. The next example shows how to obtain individual eigenvectors.

```
> with( LinearAlgebra ) :
> A := < 1 , 2 , 1 ; 4 , 0 , 5 ; 3 , 7 , -1 > ;
```

$$A := \begin{bmatrix} 1 & 2 & 1 \\ 4 & 0 & 5 \\ 3 & 7 & -1 \end{bmatrix}$$

```
> (* [2] chooses the matrix containing eigenvectors;
       [1] would choose the vector containing eigenvalues *)
> evecs := Eigenvectors( evalf( A ) )[2] :

> evecs[..,1] ;   # First eigenvector
```

$$\begin{bmatrix} 0.323515575845761 + 0.I \\ 0.656320721985336 + 0.I \\ 0.681601630043410 + 0.I \end{bmatrix}$$

```
> Norm( % , 2 ) ;
```

$$1.$$

Here, Maple has switched to hardware arithmetic (see Section 2.8), and given the entries to 15 significant figures. Note that approximately computed eigenvectors are scaled so that their Euclidean norm is 1. On the other hand, an exactly computed eigenvector is scaled so that its last nonzero entry is 1.

5.7 Solving Linear Systems

If A is a nonsingular $n \times n$ matrix and **b** is a vector with n elements, then the `LinearSolve` command can be used to find the vector **x** which satisfies the equation

$$Ax = b.$$

```
> A := < 1 , 2 , 1 ; 4 , 0 , 5 ; 3 , 7 , -1 > :
> b := < 1 , 2 , -1 > :

> with( LinearAlgebra ) :
> x := LinearSolve( A , b ) ;
```

$$x := \begin{bmatrix} -\dfrac{27}{31} \\ \dfrac{12}{31} \\ \dfrac{34}{31} \end{bmatrix}$$

```
> Norm( A . x - b , 2 ) ;   # Check solution
```
$$0$$

Note that `LinearSolve` can also be used with matrices and vectors that contain symbolic entries.

5.8 Copying Matrices and Vectors and Testing for Equality

Be careful when copying matrices and vectors; the assignment operator behaves in an 'unusual' way.

```
> U := < 1 , 2 > ;
```

$$U := \begin{bmatrix} 1 \\ 2 \end{bmatrix}$$

```
> W := U ;
```

$$W := \begin{bmatrix} 1 \\ 2 \end{bmatrix}$$

```
> W[1] := 5 :
> W[2] := 7 :
> U , W ;
```

$$\begin{bmatrix} 5 \\ 7 \end{bmatrix}, \begin{bmatrix} 5 \\ 7 \end{bmatrix}$$

After the assignment W := U, changing the elements of *W* affects *U* as well! This is because assigning an object to a new name does not create a copy. Instead it creates an extra name for the original object. Consequently, in the above example, the names *W* and *U* actually refer to the same data. To duplicate a matrix or vector, use the copy command.

```
> U := < 1 , 2 > :
> W := copy( U ) :
> W[1] := 5 :
> W[2] := 7 :
> U , W ;
```

$$\begin{bmatrix} 1 \\ 2 \end{bmatrix}, \begin{bmatrix} 5 \\ 7 \end{bmatrix}$$

An alternative method is to include the range(s) for the index (indices) on the right-hand side of the assignment, so W := copy(U) can be replaced by W := U[..] in the above example, with the same effect. The next example demonstrates that references to the same data are considered equal, but distinct matrices or vectors containing identical entries are not.

```
> u := < 1 , 2 > ;
```

$$u := \begin{bmatrix} 1 \\ 2 \end{bmatrix}$$

```
> w := u ;
```

$$w := \begin{bmatrix} 1 \\ 2 \end{bmatrix}$$

```
> evalb( u = w ) ;
```

$$\textit{true}$$

```
> y := < 1 , 2 > ;
```

$$y := \begin{bmatrix} 1 \\ 2 \end{bmatrix}$$

```
> evalb( u = y ) ;
```

$$false$$

```
> z := copy( u ) ;
```

$$z := \begin{bmatrix} 1 \\ 2 \end{bmatrix}$$

```
> evalb( u = z ) ;
```

$$false$$

```
> { u , w , y } ;
```

$$\left\{ \begin{bmatrix} 1 \\ 2 \end{bmatrix}, \begin{bmatrix} 1 \\ 2 \end{bmatrix} \right\}$$

The last statement constructs a set from the elements *u*, *w* and *y*, each of which is a vector with entries 1 and 2. Because the names *u* and *w* are references to the same data, one of these entries is deleted. However, *y* is a separate entity, and so is not deleted. The **EqualEntries** command can be used to test for equality between matrices and vectors in the usual, mathematical sense.

```
> M := < 1 , 2 ; 3 , 4 > ;
```

$$M := \begin{bmatrix} 1 & 2 \\ 3 & 4 \end{bmatrix}$$

```
> T := copy( M ) ;
```

$$T := \begin{bmatrix} 1 & 2 \\ 3 & 4 \end{bmatrix}$$

```
> evalb( T = M ) ;
```

$$false$$

```
> EqualEntries( T , M ) ;
```

$$true$$

The reason why these two different notions of equality exist is rather technical. Maple usually stores only one copy of an object, and if multiple names are associated with the same object, they must therefore point to the same memory address. This provides a very efficient way to test for equality. However, if the test is applied to duplicated matrices or vectors it will fail because the copies must be located at different addresses. The same rules apply to arrays (Section 7.5) and tables (Section 7.6), but testing for equality between objects of these types is far less common.

6

Graphics

Maple can create plots of many different kinds. To see the full range
of possibilities, execute `?PlottingGuide` to access the plotting guide.
This chapter focuses on the most common types of plot, but the principles
discussed apply to most of the others as well.

★ To export a plot, right-click on it and choose (Export). Of the available
formats, (Encapsulated Postscript) and (Portable Document Format)
are generally the best options for inclusion in a written document,
whereas (JPEG Format) and (PNG) can be used on a webpage.

6.1 Creating Basic Plots

The basic command for creating plots in Maple is `plot`.

```
> plot( x^2 ) ;
> plot( cos( theta ) ) ;
```

Here, the plotting variable (x in the first statement and θ in the second) is
determined automatically; it can also be specified explicitly by providing
a second argument to `plot`.

```
> plot( x^2 , x ) ;
> plot( cos( theta ) , theta ) ;
```

Multiple curves can be plotted by supplying the `plot` command with a
list as its first argument.

```
> plot( [ sqrt( x ) , cos( x ) , ln( x ) ] ) ;
```

Maple chooses what it thinks are sensible ranges for the axes; for the x
axis this is usually $[-10, 10]$ or, when plotting a trigonometric function,
$[-2\pi, 2\pi]$. It is also possible to explicitly set the range for either of the
axes, or both.

```
> plot( ( 1 + x ) / ( 1 - 3 * x^2 ) , x = -4 .. 4 ) ;
> plot( ( 1 + x ) / x^2 , x , y = -1 .. 1 ) ;
> plot( ( 2 - x ) / ( 1 - x )^2 , x = -4 .. 4 ,
                                      y = -1 .. 10 ) ;
```

In the second and third statements, the *y* appearing in the last argument is optional; its only effect is to set the label for the *y* axis. We could provide only the range, or use a different label. Although this syntax is intuitive (and still widely used) the preferred approach in modern versions of Maple is to set the axis labels and ranges using the `labels` and `view` options (see Section 6.2).

★ The plot command will accept a set (as opposed to a list) as its first argument, but remember that the order of the entries in a set is subject to change. For example, executing the following statement creates a red straight line and a blue parabola, which is somewhat counterintuitive.

```
> plot( { x^2 , x } , colour = [ red , blue ] ) ;
```

(See Section 6.2 for more about plot options such as `colour`.) Consequently, it is best to use a list to specify multiple curves to plot.

The `plot` command, and others such as `polarplot` (Section 6.3), `plot3d` and `contourplot` (Section 6.4), can generate graphics using functional operators (more generally, procedures) as well as expressions.

```
> plot( cos ) ;
> f := x -> x^3 :
> plot( f ) ;
```

However, mixing the two forms when plotting multiple curves is not permitted (though the `display` command introduced in Section 6.5 can be used to overcome this restriction).

```
> plot( [ cos , t^2 ] ) ;
Error, (in plot) cannot determine plotting variable
> plot( [ cos , t -> t^2 ] ) ;  # Works!
```

When a plot is generated using functional operators, the range for the independent variable, if present, must not be accompanied by a symbol.

```
> plot( exp , 0 .. 10 ) ;  # N.B. no x = before 0 .. 10
```

Instead, the `labels` option (Section 6.2) can be used to set the axis labels.

Maple evaluates arguments before passing them to plotting commands, which can lead to unexpected results if the variables have been used earlier in the worksheet. The next example creates a straight line graph, because x^2 evaluates to 9 before the plot is created.

```
> x := 3 :
> plot( x^2 ) ;
```

Explicitly specifying the plotting variable enables Maple to detect problems of this type, because prior evaluation of the arguments then produces a nonsensical result. The issue can then be resolved using unevaluation quotes.

```
> x := 3 :
> plot( x^2 , x ) ;
Error, (in plot) unexpected option: 3
> plot( 'x^2' , 'x' ) ;  # Works
```

However, the best approach is to use functional operators rather than expressions, since then there is no danger of prior evaluation.

```
> x := 3 :
> f := x -> x^2 :
> plot( f ) ;  # But not plot( f( x ) )
```

★ If a plot command fails or produces an unexpected result, consider the effect that prior evaluation has on the arguments, and use unevaluation quotes where necessary, or consider using functional operators rather than expressions.

6.2 Customising a Plot

There are many options for the `plot` command, and, since different combinations will be used in different cases, these don't need to be entered in any particular order. Instead, a '*keyword = value*' syntax is used. However, they must be placed after the functional operator(s) or expressions to be plotted and the range(s) for the variable(s) (if any).

```
> plot( 2^x , x = -1 .. 1 , colour = black ,
                            linestyle = dash ) ;
```

Both the British spelling 'colour' and the American version 'color' are acceptable here. The command to generate a plot can end up very long if multiple options are specified. To avoid this, options and their values can be stored using variables beforehand.

```
> rg := x = -5 .. 5 :
> cl := colour = [ red , blue , green ] :
> lg := legend = [ f(x) = x^2 , f(x) = x^3 ,
                                        f(x) = 1 / x^2 ] :
> lb := labels = [ x , f(x) ] :
> tl := title = "Some elementary functions" :

> plot( [ x^2 , x^3 , 1 / x^2 ] , rg , cl , lg , lb , tl ) ;
```

If the symbols used in the labels or the legend have assigned values, then it may be necessary to use unevaluation quotes to prevent prior evaluation.

```
> f := x -> x * sin( x ) + ( 3 * x - 2 ) * cos( x ) :
> plot( f , labels = [ x , f( x ) ] ) ;  # Not good
> plot( f , labels = [ x , 'f'( x ) ] ) ;
```

The **view** option can be used to set the *y* axis range for a plot.

```
> plot( x^2 , x = -5 .. 5 , view = 0 .. 10 ) ;
```

By providing **view** with a list containing two ranges, it is possible to set both the *x* and *y* axis ranges. Choosing a viewing window which extends beyond the ranges set for the curves themselves does not cause the plots themselves to extend. The viewing window is independent of the plot variables, may include all or part of the curves, and may include some empty space.

```
> vw := view = [ -0.5 * Pi .. 0.5 * Pi , -0.5 .. 0.5 ] :
> plot( [ cos , sin ] , -Pi .. Pi , vw ) ;

> vw := view = [ -2 * Pi .. 2 * Pi , -1 .. 1 ] :
> plot( [ cos , sin ] , -Pi .. Pi , vw ) ;
```

The **labels** and **view** options override any conflicting settings set using the older syntax seen in Section 6.1.

To remove vertical asymptotes from a plot, use the **discont** option.

```
> plot( 1 / ( 1 + x ) , x = -5 .. 5 , discont ) ;
```

To ensure that the same scaling is used for the x and y axes (so that circles and squares do not appear stretched), use the `scaling` option.

```
> plot( sqrt( 1 - x^2 ) , x = -1 .. 1 ,
            legend = "A semicircle" , scaling = constrained ) ;
```

A complete list of options for the `plot` command can be obtained using `?plot,options`; see also `?plot,details`.

6.3 Parametric and Polar Plots

Parametric plots are created by specifying $x(t)$ and $y(t)$, followed by the range for the parameter t, in a list.

```
> plot( [ t^3 , t , t = -5 .. 5 ] ) ;
> f := t -> 2 * cos( t ) - cos( 3 * t ) :
> plot( [ f , D( f ) , -Pi .. Pi ] ) ;
```

To plot multiple parametric curves, use a list of lists, in which each inner list contains the x and y components and parameter range for a single curve.

```
> plot( [ [ sqrt( 1 - t^2 ) , t , t = -1 .. 1 ] ,
            [ -sqrt( 1 - t^2 ) , t , t = -1 .. 1 ] ] ) ;
```

Polar coordinates can be used to create parametric plots of the form

$$(x, y) = r(\cos \theta, \sin \theta),$$

where $r = r(t)$ and $\theta = \theta(t)$.

```
> plot( [ cos( t ) , t^4 , t = 0 .. 2 ] , coords = polar ) ;
> plot( [ [ t * cos( t ) , t * sin( t ) , t = 0 .. 3 ] ,
            [ t , 1 + t^2 , t = 0 .. 2 ] ] , coords = polar ) ;
```

If a single expression (or functional operator) is provided as the first argument to a `plot` command with the `polar` option, Maple will assume that $\theta(t) = t$.

```
> plot( t^2 , coords = polar ) ;
> plot( t * cos( t ) , t = 0 .. 10 , coords = polar ) ;
```

Similarly, if a list that does not include a range for the plotting parameter is used as the first argument, Maple will assume that the elements represent $\theta(t)$ for different plots, with $r(t) = t$ in each case.

```
> plot( [ cos( t ) , sin( t ) ] , coords = polar ) ;
> plot( [ cos( t ) , sin( t ) , t = 0 .. Pi ] ,
                                    coords = polar ) ;
```

It is also possible to change the *axis* coordinates to polar.

```
> plot( log( t ) , axiscoordinates = polar ) ;
> plot( [ cos( t ) , sin( t ) , t = -Pi .. Pi ] ,
               coords = polar , axiscoordinates = polar ) ;
```

Alternatively, the `polarplot` command from the `plots` package can be used to change both the axis and variable coordinates to polar.

```
> with( plots ) :
> polarplot( t^2 ) ;
> polarplot( [ cos( t ) , sin( t ) , t = -Pi .. Pi ] ) ;
```

6.4 Three-Dimensional Plots

Surface plots can be created using the `plot3d` command.

```
> plot3d( x^2 + y^2 , x = -5 .. 5 , y = -5 .. 5 ) ;
> f := ( x , y ) -> 1 / ( 2 + sin( x + y + x * y ) ) :
> plot3d( f , -2 .. 2 , -2 .. 2 ) ;
```

The ranges were mandatory in Maple 18 and earlier, but they were made optional in Maple 2015. A very useful option when drawing surface plots is `style`, which controls how surfaces are drawn. The possible settings are `line` (a wire mesh), `point` (a discrete set of points), `pointline` (a discrete set of points joined by a wire mesh), `polygon` (shaded polygons with no outlines) and `polygonoutline` (shaded polygons with outlines). This should not be confused with `linestyle` (see Section 6.2), which controls the style of lines and has no effect if a style that does not draw lines is used. Executing the next example illustrates the difference.

```
> f := ( x , y ) -> 1 / ( 2 + sin( x + y + x * y ) ) :
> plot3d( f , -2 .. 2 , -2 .. 2 , style = line ) ;
> plot3d( f , -2 .. 2 , -2 .. 2 , style = line ,
                                    linestyle = dash ) ;

> plot3d( f , -2 .. 2 , -2 .. 2 , style = polygon ) ;
> plot3d( f , -2 .. 2 , -2 .. 2 , style = polygon ,
          linestyle = dash ) ;  # linestyle has no effect here
```

The `plots` package also provides the `contourplot` command.

```
> with( plots ) :
> contourplot( 1 / ( 1 + x^4 + y^2 ) , x = -5 .. 5 ,
                                        y = -5 .. 5 ) ;
> f := ( x , y ) -> 1 / ( 2 + sin( x + y + x * y ) ) :
> contourplot( f , -2 .. 2 , -2 .. 2 ) ;
```

This time the ranges are mandatory in versions up to and including Maple 2016. If a contour plot looks too jagged, increase the grid resolution, which is set to 25×25 by default. The number of contours can also be adjusted, or the levels (z values) at which the contours are drawn can be given in a list.

```
> f := ( x , y ) ->
    1 / sqrt( 1 + ( x^2 - 2 * x )^2 + ( y^2 - 2 * y )^2 ) :
> with( plots ) :
> gd := grid = [ 100 , 100 ] :
> contourplot( f , -3 .. 5 , -3 .. 5 , gd ) ;

> c   := contours = 20 :
> contourplot( f , -3 .. 5 , -3 .. 5 , gd , c ) ;

> c := contours = [ 0.1 , 0.5 , 0.99 ] :
> contourplot( f , -3 .. 5 , -3 .. 5 , gd , c ) ;
```

Contour plots with filled regions can also be created.

```
> with( plots ) :
> contourplot( BesselJ( 0 , x^2 + y ) , x = -2 .. 2 ,
                           y = -2 .. 2 , filledregions ) ;
```

One rather unfortunate feature of `contourplot` (and other 3D plot commands) is that some options for creating legends cannot be accessed using commands. To create a legend with an entry to describe each colour (or line style), right-click on the plot and select `Legend` ▸ `Show Legend`. Then right-click on the legend itself and select `Legend` ▸ `Edit Legend`. This process is unnecessarily time-consuming, especially when creating multiple plots with similar legends.

6.5 Combining Plots

A very flexible command for showing two or more plots on the same
axes is `display`, which is part of the `plots` package. This is particularly
useful in cases where generating everything in a single step is problematic,
e.g. if two or more curves use different coordinate systems. The next
example creates a plot of a parabola using Cartesian coordinates, and
saves this using the variable $p1$. Then a parametric plot of a spiral is
created using polar coordinates, and saved as $p2$. Finally, the two plots
are displayed on the same (Cartesian) axes.

```
> with( plots ) :
> p1 := plot( x^2 , colour = blue ) :
> p2 := plot( sqrt( t ) , t = 0 .. 25 , coords = polar ) :
> display( [ p1 , p2 ] , view = [ -5 .. 5 , -5 .. 5 ] ) ;
```

According to its help page (`?plots,display`), the `display` will com-
bine a list or set of plots, but in fact it also works with sequences, so
the square brackets in the final statement can be omitted. Note that
options which apply to the whole structure (e.g. axis ranges, labels, etc.)
can be given to `display` rather than each individual plot. Where there
is a conflict, the options to `display` take precedence. The `display`
command can also be used in conjunction with the `plottools` package,
to draw objects such as arrows, circles and spheres on a plot. The next
example creates a plot of the two functions

$$Q(x) = x^3 - 16x + 32 \quad \text{and} \quad L(x) = 3x + 2,$$

with the three intersection points shown by filled black circles. To
create these, we use a sequence of points generated by the `point`
command. This expects a list containing the x and y coordinates (or
x, y and z for a three-dimensional plot) as its first argument, and
the symbols it draws are not dependent on the scales on the axes (so
circles are not stretched). The optional arguments used here are self-
explanatory; execute `?plottools,point` for details of other options
(see also `?plot,options`).

```
> with( plots ) :
> with( plottools ) :
```

```
> Q := x -> x^3 - 16 * x + 32 :
> L := x -> 3 * x + 2 :

> # Obtain intersection x coordinates
> xc := [ solve( L( x ) = Q( x ) , x ) ] ;
```

$$xc := [-5, 2, 3]$$

```
> # Store intersection x and y coordinates
> isec := [ seq( [ x , L( x ) ] , x in xc ) ] :

> # Store points
> pts   := seq( point( xy , symbol = solidcircle ,
           symbolsize = 17 , colour = black ) , xy in isec ) :
> # Store plot
> P     := plot( [ Q , L ] ) :

> # Display combined plot
> vw    := view = [ -6 .. 6 , -100 .. 100 ] :
> display( [ P , pts ] , labels = [ x , y ] , vw ) ;
```

6.6 Plots from Data

In Maple 18 and earlier, plots were generated from numerical data using several commands, some of which have overlapping capabilities. The situation was further complicated by the fact that many of these commands accept numerical data contained in some structures, but other similar structures cause errors. Lists, vectors, matrices, lists of lists and one- and two-dimensional arrays (see Section 7.5) could be used to create some, but not all, types of plot. Maple 2015 improved this situation by introducing the **dataplot** command, which accepts data in a variety of formats and can produce many different types of plot. The old commands are still widely used, so both possibilities are shown in the examples below. To keep things simple, we will assume that data is provided in vectors and matrices, since these work with most of the old commands. The **convert**, **Matrix** and **Vector** commands can be used to create matrices and vectors from the other data structures (see Section 5.1). Many of the options for data plots are the same as the options for function plots, so they need not be discussed again here. However, it is important to note that the commands discussed below have different default options, so the results they produce may not be identical, even if they create plots of the same type. The `style` option introduced in Section 6.4, which is rarely needed with two-dimensional function plots, is important for all types of data plot, because it determines whether the data points are plotted individually or joined with lines.

A vector containing n numerical values can be interpreted as a set of y coordinates, with corresponding x coordinates $1, \ldots, n$. The following example creates plots of a 'saw-tooth' function with vertices at points

$$(1, 1), \quad (2, 2), \quad (3, 1), \quad (4, 2), \quad (5, 1) \quad \text{and} \quad (6, 2),$$

first using `dataplot`, and again using the older `listplot` command, which is part of the `plots` package.

```
> V := < 1 , 2 , 1 , 2 , 1 , 2 > :
> dataplot( V ) ;   # Maple 2015 & later
> with( plots ) :
> listplot( V ) ;
```

If we have the x and y coordinates for the points in two separate vectors, then the old command is `pointplot`. The next example draws a square with vertices $(\pm 1, \pm 1)$ using `dataplot` and then using `pointplot`. The final point is needed so that the closing edge is drawn.

```
> x_vals := < 1 ,  1 , -1 , -1 , 1 > :
> y_vals := < 1 , -1 , -1 ,  1 , 1 > :
> dataplot( x_vals , y_vals ) ;   # Maple 2015 & later
> with( plots ) :
> pointplot( x_vals , y_vals , style = line ) ;
```

The `pointplot` and `dataplot` commands will also accept point data stored in a matrix with two columns. In this case, `dataplot` needs the `points` option so that it interprets the entries in each row as an (x, y) pair, not y values for two different plots. The next example draws an isosceles triangle by the new and old methods.

```
> M := < -1 , 0 ; 1 , 0 ; 0 , 1 ; -1 , 0 > :
> dataplot( M , points ) ;   # Maple 2015 & later
> with( plots ) :
> pointplot( M , style = line ) ;
```

The simplest way to plot multiple sets of data on the same axes is to use `display`, as described in Section 6.6.

```
> with( plots ) :
> M := < 0 , 0 ; 1 , 1 ; 2 ,   4 ; 3 , 9 > :
> N := < 0 , 0 ; 1 , 3 ; 2 , -1 ; 3 , 7 > :

> # Maple 2015 & later
  p1 := dataplot( M , points , colour = red ) :
  p2 := dataplot( N , points , colour = blue ) :
  display( [ p1 , p2 ] ) ;

> p3 := pointplot( M , style = line , colour = red ) :
  p4 := pointplot( N , style = line , colour = blue ) :
  display( [ p3 , p4 ] ) ;
```

Maple also provides facilities for making three-dimensional plots from data. A matrix with three columns representing the x, y and z values can be used to create a surface plot. The next example draws a pyramid, first using **dataplot** with the **surface** option, and then using the older **surfdata** command.

```
> P := < 0 , 0 , 0 ; 0 , 1 , 0 ; 1 , 1 , 0 ;
                      1 , 0 , 0 ; 0.5 , 0.5 , 1 > ;
```

$$\begin{bmatrix} 0 & 0 & 0 \\ 0 & 1 & 0 \\ 1 & 1 & 0 \\ 1 & 0 & 0 \\ 0.5 & 0.5 & 1 \end{bmatrix}$$

```
> dataplot( P , surface ) ;  # Maple 2015 & later
> with( plots ) :
> surfdata( P ) ;
```

Grid data, where the x and y coordinates for each point are determined by its location in an $m \times n$ matrix and the entries in the matrix represent the z coordinate (so the entry in row 1 and column 1 is the z value at $(x, y) = (1, 1)$, etc.), may be used to generate a contour plot or a surface plot. The old command for contour plots from grid data is **listcontplot**, whereas **dataplot** needs the **contour** option in this case. Often a contour plot will look rather strange unless a significant amount of data is provided. However, we can use a functional operator to generate enough for a simple example.

```
> f := ( j , p ) -> ( j - 4 )^2 + ( p - 4 )^2 :
> M := Matrix( 7 , f ) ;
```

$$M := \begin{bmatrix} 18 & 13 & 10 & 9 & 10 & 13 & 18 \\ 13 & 8 & 5 & 4 & 5 & 8 & 13 \\ 10 & 5 & 2 & 1 & 2 & 5 & 10 \\ 9 & 4 & 1 & 0 & 1 & 4 & 9 \\ 10 & 5 & 2 & 1 & 2 & 5 & 10 \\ 13 & 8 & 5 & 4 & 5 & 8 & 13 \\ 18 & 13 & 10 & 9 & 10 & 13 & 18 \end{bmatrix}$$

```
> dataplot( M , contour ) ;   # Maple 2015 & later
> dataplot( M , surface ) ;   # Maple 2015 & later
> with( plots ) :
> listcontplot( M ) ;
> surfdata( M ) ;
```

★ The `dataplot` command is actually a wrapper around a number of older commands, including `contourplot`, `surfdata` and
`pointplot`. Execute `?dataplot` for the complete list. Note that
`dataplot` may reformat the data it receives before passing it on, so
simply replacing it with the more 'fundamental' command that it
ultimately uses may lead to errors.

6.7 Animations

An animation can be created from a plot which has a parameter that varies
from frame to frame (i.e. with time). The following example creates a
moving sine wave.

```
> with( plots ) :
> animate( plot , [ sin( x - t ) ,
                    x = -2 * Pi .. 2 * Pi ] , t = 0 .. Pi ) ;
```

When this is executed, Maple displays the first frame, in which $t = 0$.
Clicking on this causes the animation toolbar to appear near the top of
the window. The toolbar can be used to play the animation, pause it,
choose a frame and adjust the frame rate. Alternatively, an animation
can be controlled by right-clicking the image, hovering the cursor over
(Animation) and choosing an option from the resulting context menu.

In general, the first argument to the **animate** command must be a plot command, such as **plot**, **contourplot** or **polarplot**. The second is a list of arguments intended for use by the plot command. Finally, the animation parameter (*t* in the above example) must be specified, along with its range. The **animate** command also has a few options of its own, the most useful of which is **frames**. By default, animations contain 25 frames. The next example creates an animation with 100 frames.

```
> with( plots ) :
> c := coords = polar :
> plotargs := [ [ r , ( r + t )^2 , r = 0 .. 5 ] , c ] :
> animate( plot , plotargs , t = 0 .. 1 , frames = 100 ) ;
```

It is also possible for the animation parameter to appear in the ranges for the plot parameters, to create a curve that is traced out in time. The next example creates an animation in which the first frame contains no plot because the *x* range is initially empty. However, the axis ranges are automatically set to $[-5, 5]$ and $[0, 25]$ (the largest needed), so that only the curve changes as the animation progresses.

```
> with( plots ) :
> animate( plot , [ x^2 , x = -t .. t ] , t = 0 .. 5 ) ;
```

Three-dimensional animations can be created in much the same way; the next example creates an expanding and contracting sphere.

```
> with( plots ) :
> c := coords = spherical :
> plotargs := [ [ 0.5 + sin( t )^2 , theta , phi ] ,
                  theta = 0 .. 2 * Pi , phi = 0 .. Pi , c ] :
> animargs := t = 0 .. Pi , frames = 100 :
> animate( plot3d , plotargs , animargs ) ;
```

A special case of the **animate** command occurs when it is used with **display**. For example, suppose we wish to superimpose a moving point on a curve. We can save the curve using a variable as in Section 6.5, and the **point** command from the **plottools** package can be used to plot the point. However, the following attempt at creating the animation fails.

```
> with( plots ) :
> with( plottools ) :
> p := plot( sin , 0 .. 3 * Pi ) :
```

```
> opts := symbol = solidcircle , symbolsize = 17 ,
                                        colour = black :

> animate( display , [ p , point( [ t , sin( t ) ] ,
             opts ) , view = -1 .. 1 ] , t = 0 .. 3 * Pi ) ;
Error, (in plottools:-point) incorrect arguments for
creating points structure, try providing the dimension
option
```

The usual suspect is the root of this: the arguments to **animate** undergo prior evaluation (see Section 2.13), so that the **point** command is invoked before *t* has received a numerical value. Preventing prior evaluation resolves the issue.

```
> with( plots ) :
> with( plottools ) :
> p   := plot( sin , 0 .. 3 * Pi ) :

> opts := symbol = solidcircle , symbolsize = 17 ,
                                        colour = black :

> animate( display , [ p , 'point'( [ t , sin( t ) ] ,
             opts ) , view = -1 .. 1 ] , t = 0 .. 3 * Pi ) ;
```

Note the position of the unevaluation quotes in the last statement: **opts** needs to be evaluated before it is passed to **point**, so only the evaluation of **point** itself is deferred.

7

Programming

... the determined Real Programmer can write Fortran programs in any language.

Ed Post, 'Real Programmers Don't Use Pascal'

Most of the material considered so far involves constructing Maple worksheets that work sequentially. That is, after pressing the execute worksheet button (!!!) in the toolbar, the first line is executed, followed by the second, etc. However, it is often desirable to repeatedly execute certain statements, or to execute groups of statements only under certain conditions. In this chapter, some methods for controlling the flow of execution are considered. Some additional techniques for data storage and controlling output are also introduced. At their core, many computer languages are based on very similar ideas. Consequently, mastering programming in Maple makes learning other languages such as Fortran or C much easier.

7.1 Conditional Statements

A conditional (if) statement causes Maple to test a condition, then act differently depending on whether the condition is true or false. Such a statement begins with **if** and ends with **end if**. The latter can be abbreviated to **end** or **fi**, but the former is strongly discouraged, because several other structures can be terminated with **end**, which can lead to confusion. Attempting execution before completing the whole conditional statement will usually generate a warning, and it may generate an error. The next example shows the simplest type of conditional statement, instructing Maple to execute a sequence of statements only in cases where a simple condition is true. The line breaks shown are produced using $\boxed{\text{shift}}$ and $\boxed{\text{return}}$ (see Section 2.4). They are not necessary, but serve to improve readability, especially in complex worksheets. Likewise, there is no obligation to indent the statements between **if** and **end if**, but this makes it easier to see the structure of a worksheet, especially one that contains conditional statements nested inside one another.

```
> a := 2 :

> if a >= 0 then
    exact   := sqrt( a )   ;
    approx := evalf( exact ) ;
  end if ;
```

$$exact := \sqrt{2}$$

$$approx := 1.414213562$$

Maple displays the results because the conditional statement is itself terminated by a semicolon. No output would be produced if a colon was used here instead. Between **if** ... **then** and **end if**, colons and semicolons have no bearing on output, though they are still needed to separate statements. More information about controlling output from within conditional statements is contained in Section 7.3.

Any conditional expression can appear between **if** and **then**. When the statement is executed, Maple implicitly applies the **evalb** command to evaluate it. Therefore it is important to keep in mind that **evalf** may be needed if there is a possibility that one or both of the operands adjacent to a relational operator could be an exact symbolic value (and that **is** should be used instead if there is a danger that nearby values could lead to incorrect results; see Section 2.15 for details).

```
> s := sqrt( 2 ) ;
```

$$s := \sqrt{2}$$

```
> if s > 0 then
    "s is positive." :
  end if ;
Error, cannot determine if this expression is true or
false: 0 < 2^(1/2)
> if evalf( s ) > 0 then  # Or if is( s > 0 ) then
    "s is positive." :
  end if ;
```

$$\text{"s is positive."}$$

Boolean operators including **and**, **not** and **or** can be used to form more complicated conditional expressions for use with conditional statements.

```
> a := 13 :   # Or any other real number

> if evalf( a ) > 0 and frac( a ) = 0 then
     "a is a positive integer." :
  end if ;
```

                              "a is a positive integer."

Note the **frac** command, which extracts the fractional part of a number (execute **?frac** for more details). An **else** clause instructs Maple to take different actions (rather than none at all) if the conditional expression evaluates to *false*.

```
> a := -13 :   # Or any other real number

> if evalf( a ) > 0 then
     "a is positive." :
  else
     "a is not positive." :
  end if ;
```

                              "a is not positive."

For situations where there are three or more sets of circumstances to be accounted for, Maple provides the **elif** (else if) clause. Any number of these can be used in a conditional statement. The general structure of a conditional statement is then as follows.

```
> if first conditional expression then
     statements to execute if first conditional evaluates to true
  elif second conditional expression then
     statements to execute if first conditional evaluates to false and second
                                                       evaluates to true
  elif third conditional expression then
     statements to execute if first two conditionals evaluate to false and third
                                                       evaluates to true
       ⋮
  else
     statements to execute if all the above conditional expressions evaluate to
                                                       false
  end if :
```

Maple works downwards from `if` to `end if`, and executes the first statement sequence following a conditional expression that evaluates to *true*. If an `else` clause is included (as above), it must come after all `elif` clauses. In this case, precisely one statement sequence is always executed. Otherwise, one sequence or none may be executed. After the conditional statement has been processed, execution continues from the statement following `end if`.

7.2 Do Loops

A do loop causes Maple to repeatedly execute the same sequence of statements. The following example displays the approximate value of π six times.

```
> from 1 to 6 do
    evalf( Pi ) :
  end do ;
```

$$3.141592654$$
$$3.141592654$$
$$3.141592654$$
$$3.141592654$$
$$3.141592654$$
$$3.141592654$$

Here, output is produced at each step because the loop itself, which ends with `end do`, is followed by a semicolon. As with conditional statements, colons and semicolons inside do loops have no bearing on output (see Section 7.3 for more information). Likewise, the location of the line breaks and the indentation are for readability purposes only, and `end do` can be abbreviated to `end` or `od`, the first of which is not recommended. Attempting to execute a loop that is not properly terminated will produce a warning or an error.

For many applications, the statements inside a loop must be able to determine which step is currently being executed, and will often refer to this value in computations. This is achieved using a loop with an index variable. The next example uses an index variable j to generate the squares of the first five natural numbers.

```
> for j from 1 to 5 do
   j^2 :
   end do ;
```

$$1$$
$$4$$
$$9$$
$$16$$
$$25$$

Any Maple code can appear in the body of a do loop (between **do** and **end do**), including operations from algebra and calculus. The next example computes the (real) factorisations of $x^n - 1$ for n from 1 to 4.

```
> for n from 1 to 4 do
   factor( x^n - 1 ) :
   end do ;
```

$$(x - 1)$$
$$(x - 1)(x + 1)$$
$$(x - 1)(x^2 + x + 1)$$
$$(x - 1)(x + 1)(x^2 + 1)$$

All of the above examples could also be produced using the **seq** command from Section 2.20, but do loops offer much greater flexibility. In particular, a do loop can update a variable at each iteration. The next example uses this idea to compute a factorial. Note that the loop is terminated with a colon to prevent the display of intermediate values generated in the process of obtaining the final result.

```
> f := 1 :
> for j from 2 to 10 do
   f := f * j :   # Updates the value of f
   end do :
```

```
> f ;
```

$$3628800$$

Assuming that *start* and *finish* are numbers, the general structure of an indexed do loop of this type is as follows.

```
> for index from start to finish do
     statements
   end do :
```

Initially, the value *start* is assigned to the index variable. If **from** *start* is omitted, the initial value defaults to 1. After each iteration, the index variable is increased by 1. If the result exceeds *finish*, the loop terminates immediately. Execution then continues from the statement following **end do**, and the index variable now has the value *finish* + 1. Otherwise another iteration is performed. If *start* exceeds *finish*, the statements inside the do loop are not executed at all. Increments other than 1 are also possible, in which case the structure is as follows.

```
> for index from start by increment to finish do
    statements
  end do :
```

If *increment* is negative, the loop will terminate when *index* reaches a value that is smaller than *finish*, and will not execute at all if *finish* exceeds *start*.

```
> for j from 5 to 1 by -1 do
    j :
  end do ;
```

$$5$$
$$4$$
$$3$$
$$2$$
$$1$$

Using non-integer values for *start* or *increment* leads to a non-integer index.

```
> for x from 0 to 1 by 1 / 3 do
    x ;
  end do ;
```

$$0$$
$$\frac{1}{3}$$
$$\frac{2}{3}$$
$$1$$

This is harmless provided that exact arithmetic is used. On the other hand, creating a floating point index is highly inadvisable, because this can cause an 'off-by-one' error: one too few steps will be performed if rounding causes the index to unexpectedly exceed the final value.

```
> for x from 0 to 3 by evalf( 3 / 7 ) do
    x ;
  end do ;   # Should finish at 3...
```

$$0$$
$$0.4285714286$$
$$0.8571428572$$
$$1.285714286$$
$$1.714285715$$
$$2.142857144$$
$$2.571428573$$

```
> x ;
```

$$3.000000002$$

Sometimes it is not possible to predict how many iterations will be needed for a particular task. In these cases *finish* can be omitted, and a break statement can be used to terminate the loop. The next example finds the first natural number n such that $n! > X$, for a given X. If the conditional statement $f > X$ evaluates to *true*, the **break** command is executed and the loop terminates immediately.

```
> X := 1000000 :   # Or any other positive number
> f := 1 :

> for n from 2 do

    f := f * n :

    if f > X then
      break :
    end if :

  end do :

> n ;
```

$$10$$

It is also possible to create a do loop with no index or limits.

```
> do
     statements, including at least one break
   end do :
```

Unlimited do loops are not appropriate unless we are *absolutely* certain
that the condition(s) for a break statement will be met at some point;
otherwise Maple could enter an infinite loop. If we can't be certain, we
can impose a limit on the number of iterations, and check whether the
loop has been terminated by the break statement. For example, given a
function f and an initial value x_0, it is usually difficult to predict whether
the sequence in which $x_{j+1} = f(x_j)$ is convergent. The next example
experiments with this.

```
> f       := x -> x * sin( x ) :
> x_old := 5 :

> for j from 1 to 1000 do

      x_new := evalf( f( x_old ) ) :

      if abs( x_new - x_old ) < 0.00001 then
         break :
      end if:

      x_old := x_new :

   end do :

   if j > 1000 then
      "Loop did not break" :
   else
      "Break at step" , j , "x value:" , x_new :
   end if ;
```
$$\text{"Break at step", } 199, \text{ "x value:" } -4.714436279$$

Here, only the two most recently computed elements of the sequence are
stored at each step (storing all computed elements would be best achieved
with a table; see Section 7.6). In each iteration, there is an old value
(initially 5), from which the new value is computed. The loop terminates
if the old and new values are close together (of course this is not a
rigorous proof of convergence!). Otherwise, the new value becomes the
old value for the next iteration. If the break condition is never achieved,

j will be updated to 1001 before the loop terminates, and this is used as a test at the end.

Another useful command is **next**, which causes Maple to omit the remaining part of the current iteration, and move to the next step in a do loop. The following example displays the factorisation of natural numbers into products of prime numbers using the **ifactor** command. Steps where the index is itself prime are omitted.

```
> for j from 2 to 10 do

    if isprime( j ) then
       next :
    end if :

    j , ifactor( j ) :

  end do ;
```

$$4, (2)^2$$
$$6, (2)(3)$$
$$8, (2)^3$$
$$9, (3)^2$$
$$10, (2)(5)$$

The same effect could be achieved using a conditional statement to prevent Maple from attempting a factorisation when the index is prime. However, in more complex cases this approach may necessitate enclosing large blocks of statements between **if** and **end if**, so the implementation using **next** is often simpler.

A while clause is a less flexible alternative to a break statement. Whereas any number of break statements can occur anywhere in a do loop, a while clause is always checked immediately before the start of each iteration, after the index (if any) has been set in the first step or updated in subsequent steps. While clauses offer nothing that cannot be achieved using break statements, and are prone to off-by-one errors if used without due care. Nevertheless, they often appear in Maple worksheets, so it's worth considering them. The following example shows a flawed attempt to find the first factorial that exceeds 1000 (see page 153 for a solution to the same problem using a break statement).

```
> f := 1 :
  for n from 2 while f <= 1000 do
    f := f * n :
  end do :

> n ;
```

$$8$$

The correct answer is 7, but *n* is updated to 8 *before* the test on *f* is applied. One way to avoid this is to separate the index from the loop.

```
> f := 1 :
> n := 1 :

> while f <= 1000 do
    n := n + 1 :
    f := f * n :
  end do :

> n ;
```

$$7$$

Now it's clear that the update to *n* takes place after the test on *f*.

A range of characters can be used for the index in a do loop. The default behaviour is then to step forward one place in the alphabet in each iteration, but this can be changed by setting a different increment.

```
> s := "" :

> for c from "z" to "a" by -1 do
    s := cat( s , c ) :
  end do :

> s ;
```

$$\text{"zyxwvutsrqponmlkjihgfedcba"}$$

As with loops over numeric ranges, there is a final update to the index after the last iteration.

```
> for s from "a" to "d" do
    s :
  end do ;
```

```
                              "a"
                              "b"
                              "c"
                              "d"
> s ;

                              "e"
```

It is also possible to loop over the entries in a larger structure, such as a list or vector. The following example sums the odd entries in the list *L*, using the type operator : : introduced in Section 2.21 to distinguish these from the even entries.

```
> L := [ 1 , 2 , 4 , 8 , 25 ] :
> s := 0 :

> for j in L do

    if j :: odd then
      s := s + j :
    end if :

  end do :

> s ;

                              26
```

Similarly, it is possible to loop over the characters in a string.

```
> for c in "toad" do
    c ;
  end do ;
                              "t"
                              "o"
                              "a"
                              "d"
> c ;

                              "d"
```

The result of the last statement shows that there is no extra increment to the index at the end of a loop that uses the **in** operator.

★ Assignments can be made to an index variable from inside a do loop. This is rarely a good idea, because it may cause Maple to become trapped in an infinite loop.

```
> for j from 1 to 10 do
     j := 5 :
   end do ;  # Don't execute this!
```

Of course, setting *j* to 10 (or a larger value) would terminate the loop at the end of the first step, but using a break statement is generally a better way to make an early exit.

7.3 Nesting and printlevel

When loops and conditional statements are *nested* (placed one inside another), there are two factors to consider in determining which statements will produce output. First, only the termination of the outermost end do or end if affects output. A colon here ensures that none of the statements inside have their results displayed. The situation is slightly more complicated if a semicolon is used. In this case, the results of statements at which the *nesting level* does not exceed the current value of the printlevel environment variable will be displayed. The default value for printlevel is 1. Outside any do loops and conditional statements (also procedures; see Section 8.8) the nesting level is 0. Each time Maple enters a do loop or conditional statement, the nesting level increases by 1, and it decreases by 1 at the end. The next example uses a do loop along with the isprime command to display prime numbers less than 20.

```
> printlevel := 2 :

> for j from 2 to 20 do

     if isprime( j ) then
        j :
     end if :

   end do ;
```

$$2$$
$$3$$
$$5$$
$$7$$
$$11$$
$$13$$
$$17$$
$$19$$

The last line is terminated by a semicolon, but the innermost statement has nesting level 2, because it is inside a conditional statement, which is itself inside a do loop. Therefore it is necessary to set `printlevel` to 2 (or a larger value), or else no output will be produced.

★ Setting a high value for `printlevel` causes Maple to display information about the inner workings of some of its own procedures. However, commands that form part of the kernel (see Section 8.10) are not affected by `printlevel`.

```
> printlevel := 25 :
> add( p^2 , p = 1 .. 3 ) ;   # add is a kernel command
```
$$14$$
```
> sum( 1 / p^2 , p = 1 .. infinity ) ;
                          # Produces a lot of output
```

7.4 The print and printf Commands

Often there is no value for `printlevel` which produces exactly the desired output; all produce either too much or too little. The `print` command can be used to explicitly tell Maple what to display. It is not affected by the value of `printlevel`. The next example looks for Pythagorean triples, that is, integers a, b and c such that

$$c = \sqrt{a^2 + b^2}.$$

When a triple is found, a, b and c are printed. Had we tried to do this by increasing `printlevel` to 3, the statement which calculates c would generate a great deal of unwanted output, since it has nesting level 2.

```
> N := 20 :   # Or any other natural number

> for a from 3 to N do   # Why start from 3?
    for b from a + 1 to N do

      c := sqrt( a^2 + b^2 ) :

      if c :: integer then
        print( a , b , c ) :
      end if :

    end do :
  end do :
```

$$3, 4, 5$$
$$5, 12, 13$$
$$6, 8, 10$$
$$8, 15, 17$$
$$9, 12, 15$$
$$12, 16, 20$$
$$15, 20, 25$$

Finer control over *how* the output is displayed can be achieved using the `printf` command. This is similar to `print`, but it takes a *format specification string* as its first argument. For example, the string "%2d %2d %2d\n" tells Maple to expect three integers to display, and to use two character columns for each with one space in between, so that single- and two-digit numbers line up neatly. The last part of the format specification (\n) tells Maple to begin a new line. In the previous example, `print( a , b , c )` could be replaced by `printf( "%2d %2d %2d \n" , a , b , c )`, leading to the following (somewhat neater) result.

```
 3  4  5
 5 12 13
 6  8 10
 8 15 17
 9 12 15
12 16 20
15 20 25
```

The most important elements used to make up format specification strings are summarised in Table 7.1. In general, allowing more characters than

Element	Meaning
%a	An algebraic expression.
%*j*a	An algebraic expression to be displayed using *j* characters.
%d	An integer.
%*j*d	An integer to be displayed using *j* characters.
%e	A floating point number to be displayed in scientific notation with 6 digits after the decimal point in the mantissa.
%*j*e	A floating point number to be displayed in scientific notation using *j* characters, with 6 digits after the decimal point in the mantissa.
%*j*.*p*e	A floating point number to be displayed in scientific notation using *j* characters, with *p* digits after the decimal point in the mantissa.
%f	A floating point number to be displayed in decimal format with 6 digits after the decimal point.
%*j*f	A floating point number to be displayed in decimal format using *j* characters, with 6 digits after the decimal point.
%*j*.*p*f	A floating point number to be displayed in decimal format using *j* characters, with *p* digits after the decimal point.
\n	Begin a new line.
%s	A string.
%*j*s	A string to be displayed using *j* characters.

Table 7.1 *Elements of format specification strings and their meanings. Decimal points and the symbols +, − and e all count toward the total number of characters used.*

necessary causes Maple to pad the output with leading spaces or trailing zeros so that everything lines up properly. When displaying a numerical value, omitting the number of places to show after the decimal point causes this to default to six. If a format specification does not set a maximum number of characters, Maple will simply use as many as it needs. If too few character columns are specified then the output is still produced, but it may not line up as expected.

```
> a := 123.456   :
> b := 1234.5678  :
> c := 12345.6789 :
> printf( "%8f\n%8f\n%8f\n" , a , b , c ) ;
123.456000
1234.567800
12345.678900
```

Exact values such as π and $\sqrt{2}$ are automatically approximated when used in this context (so there is no need to use `evalf`), but otherwise data whose type does not match the format specification string causes an error.

```
> printf( "%12f\n%12f" , Pi , sqrt( 2 ) ) ;
     3.141593
     1.414214
> printf( "%12d \n" , Pi ) :
Error, (in fprintf) integer expected for integer format
```

Execute `?printf` for more details about the `printf` command.

When `print` is used to display a string, the surrounding quotes appear in the output.

```
> print( "Don't quote me." ) ;
```
$$\text{"Don't quote me."}$$

One way to avoid this is to use name quotes (see Section 2.12).

```
> print( `Don't quote me.` ) ;
```
$$\textit{Don't quote me.}$$

This was common practice in very old versions of Maple, which had no string type (this was introduced in Maple V release 5). It is difficult to conceive an example in which it causes a problem, but there is no longer any reason to use names in this way. Instead, formatting the output using the more powerful `printf` command is recommended.

```
> printf( "%s" , "Don't quote me." ) ;
Don't quote me.
```

7.5 Arrays

An array is similar to a vector or a matrix (see Chapter 5), but it can have up to 63 dimensions, and the lower limit for the indices does not have to be 1. Executing the following statement creates an array A with six rows, numbered from 0 to 5, and three columns, numbered from -1 to 1.

```
> A := Array( 0 .. 5 , -1 .. 1 ) :
```

Note the capital A in **Array**, which is important. The older command **array** has been deprecated, and should not be used in new worksheets. By default, arrays are filled with zeros. The entries can be initialised to another value using the **fill** option.

```
> A := Array( 1 .. 3 ) ;
```

$$A := [0 \ 0 \ 0]$$

```
> B := Array( 1 .. 4 , fill = Pi ) ;
```

$$B := [\pi \ \pi \ \pi \ \pi]$$

Arrays can also be generated from other structures such as lists, vectors and matrices using the **Array** command, or the **convert** command.

```
> C := Array( 1 .. 3 , [ a , b , c ] ) ;
```

$$C := [a \ b \ c]$$

```
> E := Array( [ [ 1 , 2 ] , [ 3 , 4 ] ] ) ;
```

$$E := \begin{bmatrix} 1 & 2 \\ 3 & 4 \end{bmatrix}$$

```
> F := convert( < s , t , w > , Array , 1 .. 3 ) ;
```

$$E := [s \ t \ w]$$

Where an array is formed from another structure, omitting the ranges causes the starting point for the indices to default to 1.

Obviously, Maple cannot conveniently display the contents of an array with more than two dimensions on a two-dimensional screen. There are two additional constraints that apply to the display of one- and two-dimensional arrays. First, the contents will not be displayed if the size in any dimension exceeds **rtablesize** (cf. matrices and vectors, Section 5.3). Second, if the indices do not all start from 1, Maple will display their ranges, and a set containing nonzero entries and their corresponding indices. Maple 18 will also display a number of options associated with the array in this case. To display an array with an index that does not start from 1 in the usual format, simply convert it to a matrix or vector.

```
> B := Array( 3 .. 5 , [ 2 , 6 , 0 ] ) ;
```

$$B := Array\,(3..5, \ \{3 = 2, 4 = 6\})$$

```
> Vector( B ) ;
```

$$[2\ 6\ 0]$$

The elements of an array can be accessed using an index (or sequence of indices) in square brackets.

```
> C := Array( [ [ d , e ] , [ f , g ] ] ) ;
```

$$C := \begin{bmatrix} d & e \\ f & g \end{bmatrix}$$

```
> C[1,2] ;
```

$$e$$

```
> C[2,1] ;
```

$$f$$

```
> E := Array( -1 .. 1 , [ 2 , 4 , 7 ] ) :
> E[0] ;
```

$$4$$

```
> E[1] ;
```

$$7$$

As described in Section 2.18 (see also Section 5.2), ranges can be used to access or set several elements simultaneously.

```
> A := Array( 1 .. 3 , 1 .. 3 ) :
> A[1,1..2] := 7  :
> A[2,..]    := Pi :
> A[3,2..]   := k  :
> A ;
```

$$\begin{bmatrix} 7 & 7 & 0 \\ \pi & \pi & \pi \\ 0 & k & k \end{bmatrix}$$

```
> A[..,2] ;
```

$$[7\ \pi\ k]$$

Similarly, all or part of an array can be overwritten by the entries from another array, or from a matrix or a vector. However, using a list in this way will produce the same effect as in Section 5.2: the whole list will be copied into each position.

```
> A := Array( 1 .. 5 ) :
> v := < a , b , c > :
> L := [ P , Q ] :
> A[1..3] := v :
> A[4..5] := L :
> A ;
```

$$[a\ b\ c\ [P,Q]\ [P,Q]]$$

```
> A[4..5] := Array( L ) :
> A ;
```

$$[a\ b\ c\ P\ Q]$$

The **upperbound** and **lowerbound** commands are used to enquire about the bounds for the indices, so there is no need to keep track of them manually.

```
> A := Array( -5 .. 5 ) :
> lowerbound( A ) ;
```

$$-5$$

```
> upperbound( A ) ;
```

$$5$$

For an array with more than one dimension, the default is to return a sequence in which the nth entry is the bound in the nth dimension. Alternatively, a second argument can be used to obtain the bound in a particular dimension.

```
> B := Array( -4 .. 4 , 1 .. 3 ) :
> upperbound( B ) ;
```

$$4, 3$$

```
> lowerbound( B ) ;
```

$$-4, 1$$

```
> upperbound( B , 1 ) ;
```

$$4$$

```
> lowerbound( B , 2 ) ;
```

$$1$$

The **upperbound** and **lowerbound** commands can also be used with lists, sets, vectors and matrices, but remember that the lower bound for these structures is always 1.

Using parentheses to access array elements has a different effect from using square brackets. The actual index ranges are ignored, and the elements are assumed to be numbered starting from 1. For example, if *A* is a one-dimensional array, then A(1) always refers to the first element.

```
> A := Array( -1 .. 1 , [ a , b, c ] ) :
> A[1] ;
```
$$c$$

```
> A(1) ;
```
$$a$$

An assignment to an out of range element will cause the array to expand if parentheses are used for the index, whereas it causes an error if square brackets are used.

```
> A := Array( -1 .. 1 , fill = a ) :
> A(4) := 7 :   # But not A[2] := 7 :
> Vector( A ) ;  # Display the contents of the array
```
$$[a\ a\ a\ 7]$$

```
> A[2] ;
```
$$7$$

Negative indices for array entries should be used with extreme caution. If the lower bound for the index of a one-dimensional array *A* is 1, then A[-1] and A[-2] refer to the last entry, and the penultimate entry, etc. just as they do for a set or list (see Section 2.18). However, if the lower bound is not 1, then A[-j] refers to the entry in position $-j$ (which may not actually exist).

```
> A := Array( [ a , b , c ] ) :
> A[-1] ;
```
$$c$$

```
> B := Array( -1 .. 1 , [ a , b , c ] ) :
> B[-1] ;
```
$$a$$

```
> B[-2] ;
Error, Array index out of range
```

For a multidimensional array, backwards referencing using negative indices works if the lower bound in all dimensions is 1. To get around these issues, use parentheses rather than square brackets, since then the entries are assumed to be numbered from 1.

```
> A := Array( [ a , b , c ] ) :
> A(-1) ;
```

$$c$$

```
> B := Array( -1 .. 1 , [ a , b , c ] ) :
> B(-1) ;
```

$$c$$

```
> B(-2) ;
```

$$b$$

As with matrices and vectors (see Section 5.8), assigning an array to a new name creates an extra name for the same array, not a copy. When a copy is required, the copy command can be used, or the range(s) for the index (indices) can be provided on the right-hand side of the assignment.

```
> A := Array( 1 .. 3 , fill = a ) :
> B := copy( A ) :   # or B := A[..] but not B := A :

> B[1] := 7 :
> # Display the contents of the arrays
> Vector( A ) , Vector( B ) ;
```

$$[a\ a\ a],\ [7\ a\ a]$$

★ Although there is no substantive difference between a two-dimensional array and a matrix, some linear algebra commands will not work with arrays. Conversion to a matrix solves this problem.

```
> A := Array( [ [ -2 , 1 ] , [ 1 , 0 ] ] ) :
> with( LinearAlgebra ) :
> MatrixInverse( Matrix( A ) ) ;
                              # But not MatrixInverse( A )
```

$$\begin{bmatrix} 0 & 1 \\ 1 & 2 \end{bmatrix}$$

7.6 Tables

A table is another type of indexed data structure, with properties very different from those of the array. The index need not be an integer, and there is no need to define a range of valid indices at the outset. Instead, entries are inserted into the table as necessary.

```
> T     := table() :
> T[Pi] := 7 ;
```

$$T_\pi := 7$$

```
> T[A]  := exp( 1 ) ;
```

$$T_A := e$$

```
> T[Pi] , T[A] ;
```

$$7, e$$

Parentheses cannot be used to access the elements of a table. A very important property of tables is that indices that have not been associated with an entry trigger an unevaluated return.

```
> W := table() :
> W[1] ;
```

$$W_1$$

In this respect, the entries in a table behave like ordinary variables, unlike the elements of an array, which always have a value. Consequently, **unassign** can be used to remove an entry from a table.

```
> t := table() :
> t[1] := 10 :
> t[2] := 27 :
> t[1] , t[2] ;
```

$$10, 27$$

```
> unassign( 't[1]' ) :
> t[1] , t[2] ;
```

$$t_1, 27$$

Similarly, **assigned** can be used to check whether a particular entry is in use.

```
> w      := table() :
> w[1]  := 24 :
> assigned( w[1] ) ;
```

true

```
> assigned( w[2] ) ;
```

false

Automatic insertion of table elements is useful in circumstances where we need to work with a sequence of values, but don't know a priori how many such values are needed. Tables are also useful in situations where we need to store data that doesn't naturally fit into a rectangular structure such as an array or a matrix (see Section 9.1 for an example), and in cases where a sequence of names of the form $c_0, c_1, c_2, \ldots$ is more practical than $a, b, c, \ldots$ For example, a polynomial with arbitrary coefficients, which can be assigned values at a later stage, can be generated as follows.

```
> n := 8 :  # Or any other natural number
```

```
> c := table() :
> poly := add( c[j] * x^j , j = 0 .. n ) ;
```

$$poly := c_8 x^8 + c_7 x^7 + c_6 x^6 + c_5 x^5 + c_4 x^4 + c_3 x^3 + c_2 x^2 + c_1 x + c_0$$

Had we used an array here, the values of the coefficients c_j would need to be set before defining `poly`. A more complex example that exploits this facility is given in Section 9.5.

★ If no indexed data structure T exists, an assignment to `T[k]` automatically creates a table.

```
> T[1] := 2 :
> Describe( T ) ;
```

```
T::table = table([(1)=2])
```

However, explicitly creating the table with the **table** command makes it easier to locate the first place at which it is used, and this can be helpful when debugging a complex worksheet.

Tables use last name evaluation (see Section 2.13), which means that a name assigned to a table evaluates to itself.

```
> T    := table() :
> T[1] := 5 :
> T ;
```

$$T$$

To see the contents of a table, use **Describe**, or force full evaluation using **eval**.

```
> T    := table() :
> T[1]  := 3 :
> T[Pi] := 12 :
> Describe( T ) ;

T::table = table([(1)=3,(Pi)=12])

> eval( T ) ;
```

$$table([1 = 3, \pi = 12])$$

Alternatively, the indices and corresponding entries can be displayed separately.

```
> W := table() :
> W[a] := Pi :
> W[1] := k  :
> W[2] := 27 :
> indices( W ) ;
```

$$[1], [2], [a]$$

```
> entries( W ) ;
```

$$[k], [27], [\pi]$$

★ The **seq**, **add** and **mul** commands can be used with tables, but the last name evaluation barrier must be broken using **eval**.

```
> T := table() :
> T[a] := 5  :
> T[b] := 10 :
> add( c , c in T ) ;
```

$$T$$

```
> add( c , c in eval( T ) ) ;
```
$$15$$

The last statement can be abbreviated to `add( eval( T ) )` in Maple 2015 and later.

An application of `eval` is also needed to cause `whattype` to check whether a name has been associated with a table. However, it is possible to check this using `type` in the usual way.

```
> T := table() :
> whattype( T ) ;
```
symbol
```
> whattype( eval( T ) ) ;
```
table
```
> type( T , table ) ;
```
true

As the next example shows, `Describe` will report that a table is a package if none of its indices are integers (remember that objects in Maple can possess more than one type).

```
> T     := table() :
> T[k] := 1 :
> Describe( T ) ;
```

package T:

```
    k::integer = 1
```

```
> whattype( eval( T ) ) ;
```
table
```
> T[1] := 3 :
> Describe( T ) ;
```

T::table = table([(1)=3,(k)=1])

This discrepancy between `whattype` and `Describe` does not appear to have any adverse consequences.

The type table help page (`?type,table`) contains no mention of checking entry types, and indeed the normal syntax for this (taking into account the fact that there is a command `table`; see Section 2.21) does not work, though it does not produce an error.

```
> T := table() :
> T[1] := 5 :
> type( T , 'table( numeric )' ) ;
```
$$false$$

Bizarrely, omitting the unevaluation quotes *does* seem to work.

```
> T := table() :
> W := table() :
> T[a] := 1 :
> T[b] := 5 :
> W[1] := "abc" :
> W[2] := "def" :
> type( T , table( numeric ) ) ;
```
$$true$$

```
> type( T , table( string ) ) ;
```
$$false$$

```
> type( W , table( numeric ) ) ;
```
$$false$$

```
> type( W , table( string ) ) ;
```
$$true$$

Quite why this happens is unclear: Maplesoft technical support would only say that the syntax is unsupported, and not guaranteed to work in all cases. A safer approach is to use `type( T , tabular( numeric ) )` to determine whether *T* is a tabular object containing only numerical entries. This will also return *true* if *T* is an array, matrix or vector containing only numerical entries, but it can be used alongside `type( T , table )` where necessary.

```
> T    := table() :
> T[1] := 2 :
> type( T , tabular( string ) ) and type( T , table ) ;
```
$$false$$

```
> type( T , tabular( numeric ) ) and type( T , table ) ;
```

$$true$$

Placing a table name on the right-hand side of an assignment operator creates an assignment chain (see Section 2.13).

```
> T     := table() :
> S     := T :
> S ;
```

$$T$$

```
> eval( S ) ;
```

$$table([\ ])$$

Since there is no meaningful way to define a range for a table index, the copy command is the only convenient way to duplicate a table.

```
> T    := table() :
> T[1] := 7 :
> W     := copy( T ) :  # But not W := T :
> T[2] := 5 :
> Describe( W ) ;

W::table = table([(1)=7])

> Describe( T ) ;

T::table = table([(1)=7,(2)=5])
```

Note that using **eval** to break through the last name evaluation barrier with an assignment such as W := **eval**(T) would create another name for the original table, not a copy (cf. matrices and vectors in Section 5.8).

8

Procedures

I haven't seen you before. Are you local?

Tubbs Tattsyrup, 'The League of Gentlemen'

Section 3.4 explained how to define simple mathematical functions using arrow notation. A procedure is similar, but it can use any Maple code to obtain its results, including conditional statements and do loops. In fact, a functional operator is a special case of a procedure. Procedures provide a means to split complex worksheets into simpler parts, and to avoid the need to repeat statements. In this chapter, the most common and important features of procedures are introduced. For a more complete account, see Chapter 6 of the Programming Guide (`?ProgrammingGuide,chapter06`).

★ It is important to search the help system before writing a procedure, to check whether the required functionality is provided by the Maple library. Indeed, the range of features in Maple is so wide that finding short instructive programming examples that do something new is very difficult in some cases. Consequently, the `harmonic_number` procedure in Section 8.9, the `contains_char` procedure in Section 8.6 and the sorting procedure in Section 9.4 all provide functionality that is already available (execute `?harmonic`, `?StringTools,Search` and `?sort` for details).

8.1 A Basic Procedure

The next example shows a basic (and rather trivial) procedure called `double`. The procedure definition begins with the `proc` keyword, and ends with `end proc`, which can be abbreviated to `end`, though this is not recommended (cf. `end if` in Section 7.1). The location of the line breaks and the indentation of the statement inside the procedure are for readability purposes only. The statement in which the procedure definition is assigned to the name **double** needs to be executed before the procedure can be used. When this occurs, Maple displays the procedure definition because **end proc** is terminated with a semicolon. The amount of output displayed in these circumstances can be reduced by setting the **verboseproc** interface variable to 0 (see Section 8.10), but in any case displaying a procedure definition in the output immediately after it appears in the input is rarely useful. Therefore a colon will be used to terminate subsequent procedure definitions.

```
> double := proc( x )

    return 2 * x :

  end proc ;
```
$$double := \mathbf{proc}(x)\ \mathbf{return}\ 2 * x\ \mathbf{end\ proc}$$
```
> a := 1 :
> double( a ) ;  # First test
```
$$2$$
```
> 16 + double( 5 ) ;  # Second test
```
$$26$$

The **double** procedure takes a single *argument* as its input. For the first test this is *a* and in the second it is 5. The argument is first evaluated and then *bound* to the *parameter* x. This means that, wherever the parameter x appears inside the procedure, it is literally replaced by the result of evaluating the argument (1 in the first test and 5 in the second). The procedure terminates when execution reaches the **return** command. The result of the procedure is specified by the value that appears between the **return** command and the colon terminating the return statement ($2x$ here). A procedure can also have multiple return values, or none; see Section 8.6 for more details. After the procedure terminates, execution continues from the point at which it was invoked. The following steps take place when the statement **double(a)** is executed.

• The argument *a* is evaluated to 1.

- The **double** procedure is invoked, with 1 in place of *x*.
- The procedure is terminated by the statement **return 2 * x**, causing it to return 2 as its result.

The return value should not be confused with the output displayed on the screen (see Section 2.7). When **double(a)** is executed, the return value is displayed because this is the result of the *statement*. On the other hand, when the last statement is executed, the result of **double(5)** is computed, returned, and added to 16. The result of the *statement* is displayed, not the return value of the procedure.

★ If Maple reports an error when a procedure definition is executed, this is probably caused by a syntax problem such as a missing (semi)colon. The set of possible locations for the error can be narrowed down by deactivating sections of code using # or (* and *) (see Section 2.4), and executing the definition again.

★ When writing a procedure, keep the definition in an executable state: after typing **proc(...)**, **do** or **if ... then**, insert the corresponding **end proc**, **end do** or **end if** immediately. This way, an unfinished procedure definition can be executed to check for syntax errors each time a few lines are added.

★ If Maple unexpectedly returns an expression unevaluated, check that all necessary procedure definitions have been executed.

8.2 The Structure of a Procedure

For the purposes of this book, a Maple procedure definition has the following general structure (the return type declaration, which is relatively unimportant in Maple, is omitted).

> *procedure name* := **proc(** *parameter sequence* **)**

    description
    option declarations
    local and global declarations

    statement sequence

end proc :

The description, declarations and statement sequence are optional, and each can be used or not as appropriate. It is generally good practice to give each procedure a descriptive name, and to include a brief explanation of what it does and (if this is not obvious) how. This makes it easier to reuse the procedure at a later date. Comments can be used for this purpose, but it is better to use the purpose-built description facility because the information will then be shown when `Describe` is used.

```
> my_proc := proc()

    description "A very nice procedure" :

    end proc :

> Describe( my_proc ) ;

# A very nice procedure
my_proc( )
```

To save space, the description is omitted from subsequent examples in this chapter, since the purpose of the procedures is explained in the text. The other elements that make up a procedure are more complex, and will be discussed throughout this chapter. It is not practical to consider each in isolation, due to the way in which they interact. The order in which the description and option, local and global declarations appear does not matter (though in the author's view it makes sense for the description to appear first of all). However, if any of these elements are present then they must appear before the statement sequence, which makes up the remainder of the procedure. The next example shows a very common syntax error related to this.

```
> my_proc := proc() :

    option remember :

    end proc :
Error, reserved word `option` or `options` unexpected
```

The problem here is caused by the colon immediately after `proc()`, which should not be present. Its effect is to create an empty statement, and, since this is not an option, global or local declaration, Maple treats it as part of the statement sequence. Therefore the requirement on the ordering of statements is violated, leading to an error.

8.3 Local and Global Variables

Procedures can have their own internal variables, which cannot be accessed from elsewhere in the worksheet. These are called *local* variables. Variables elsewhere in the worksheet with the same name are separate entities. In the next example, the `truncated_exp` procedure computes the sum

$$e_n(x) = \sum_{j=0}^{n} \frac{x^j}{j!}.$$

To do this, it uses local variables s and j to serve as a running total and a loop index, respectively. The `local` keyword is used to declare the existence of these variables. There are also variables called s and j outside the procedure, but these are separate entities, so their values do not change either when the procedure is defined or when it is used.

```
> s := 25 :
> j := Pi :
> truncated_exp := proc( x , n )

    local s , j :

    s := 1 :

    for j from 1 to n do
      s := s + x^j / j! :
    end do :

    return s :

  end proc :

> truncated_exp( 1.3 , 100 ) ;
                        3.669296667

> s , j ;
                          25, π
```

The fact that multiple variables with the same name can exist may seem confusing at first, but it's important to keep in mind that a complex project may use a very large number of procedures. Keeping track of which names have been used and how the data they refer to might be affected by procedure calls would be very difficult (and annoying) in such circumstances. Instead, local variables allow the internal operations of each procedure to be independent from the rest of the worksheet.

Variables that are not local are said to be *global*. Only one global variable with each name can exist in a worksheet. It can be accessed from inside a procedure using the `global` keyword. The next example shows a direct comparison between the behaviour of local and global variables.

```
> local_global_demo := proc()

    local  a :
    global b :

    print( a , b ) :
    a := 1 : b := 2 :
    print( a , b ) :

    return :

  end proc :
> a := Pi : b := Pi :
> local_global_demo() ;
```
$$a, \pi$$
$$1, 2$$

```
> a , b ;
```
$$\pi, 2$$

```
> local_global_demo() ;
```
$$a, 2$$
$$1, 2$$

Here, there are two objects called a: the global variable, which exists outside the procedure, and the local variable, which is only visible inside. Before the procedure is used, the global a is assigned the value π. However, in the two **print** commands, a refers to the local variable. In the first instance this has not been assigned a value, so *a* is printed. In the second, *a* has the value 1. Since the penultimate statement is outside the procedure, it refers to the global *a*, whose value is still π. When the procedure is invoked for a second time, the local *a* is again undefined at the first `print` statement. It does not retain the value 1 because new instances of local variables are created each time a procedure is used, and discarded when it terminates. On the other hand, the statement `global b` tells Maple that occurrences of *b* inside and outside the procedure refer to the same entity. Thus, when the first `print` command is executed, *b* has the value π. The subsequent assignment to *b* globally changes its value. The penultimate statement demonstrates that the value of *b* outside the procedure has indeed changed from π to 2, and it still has this value when the procedure is invoked again. This behaviour can lead to errors, because it is easy to forget which global variables are affected by which procedures. In most cases, there are much better ways to share information with the rest of the worksheet. See Sections 8.4 and 8.6 for details.

★ A procedure should not access or (worse) change data via the `global` keyword unless this is *absolutely necessary*.

★ If a variable is used in a procedure but is not declared to be either local or global, Maple automatically declares it global, unless it appears on the left-hand side of an assignment, or as the index variable in a do loop. In these last two cases, Maple will automatically declare it local and issue a warning.

★ Variables can be assigned values as part of a `global` or `local` declaration. For example, in a procedure that contains the declaration `local j := 1` the local variable *j* will be assigned the initial value 1 each time the procedure is executed.

Local variables are subject to one-level evaluation rules. This means that chains of assignments are not automatically followed to the end, as they are for global variables (see Section 2.13). When the `print` command in the next example is executed, *d* evaluates to *c*, but *c* does not further evaluate to 1.

```
> my_proc := proc()

   local c , d :

   d := c :
   c := 1 :

   print( d ) :

   return :

   end proc :
> my_proc() ;
```

$$c$$

One way around this is to force a full evaluation by using **eval**, but the issue can be avoided entirely by placing the assignment to c before the assignment to *d*. In fact, there are very few situations in which one-level evaluation problems cannot be avoided by arranging the statements in a procedure in a more logical order.

Another important property of local variables is that they may 'escape' from a procedure. In the next example, the unevaluation quotes cause the name *a* to be returned, as opposed to its value 1. The next time this *escaped local variable* occurs in a context that causes evaluation, it evaluates to 1. None of this affects the fact that the global *a* has been assigned the value 32 outside the procedure, so we briefly have a situation in which two variables with the name *a* and different values are in existence in the main part of the worksheet. However, in this case, the escaped local variable is both short-lived and harmless.

```
> a := 32 :
> my_proc := proc()

   local a := 1 :

     return 'a' :

   end proc :
```

```
> my_proc() ;
```

$$a$$

```
> % ;
```

$$1$$

```
> a ;
```

$$32$$

Let us now consider an example in which naive programming leads to more serious problems with one-level evaluation rules and escaped locals.

```
> my_proc := proc( x )

    local p , y , t :

    p := y^2 + 1 :
    y := t + 1 :

    # 2nd argument should be eval( p )
    return subs( t = x , p ) :

  end proc :

> my_proc( z ) ;
```

$$y^2 + 1$$

```
> evalb( % = y^2 + 1 ) ;
```

$$\textit{false}$$

Before the **subs** command is executed, its second argument, p, evaluates to $y^2 + 1$ but y does not evaluate to $t + 1$ (as it would if p were global). Consequently, the substitution fails, and $y^2 + 1$ is returned, and not $(z + 1)^2 + 1$ as might have been expected. To make matters worse, the y in the returned expression is an escaped local, so it is not the same as the symbol y used outside the procedure. These problems can be prevented either by using **eval**, or by making the assignment to y before the assignment to p. Escaped local variables can also be created when an object that uses last name evaluation is returned as the result of a procedure. Consider the following example, in which the local variable *t* is associated with a table.

```
> my_proc := proc()

    local t := table() :

    t[1] := 5 :

    return t :   # Should be return eval( t ) :

  end proc :
> w := my_proc() :
> w[1] ;
```

$$5$$

```
> w ;
```

$$t$$

```
> t[1] ;
```

$$t_1$$

When the procedure is executed, the name *t* is returned as its result, and assigned as the value of *w*. The elements of the table can be accessed through its association with *w*, so w[1] evaluates to 5. However, *w* itself evaluates to *t*, and, because *t* is an escaped local variable, it cannot be accessed outside the procedure in any other way. Consequently, when the last statement is executed, t[1] does not refer to a table entry, and evaluates to itself. To prevent this slightly confusing situation, we should use **return eval(t)** to ensure that the table (and not its name) is returned.

8.4 Arguments and Parameters

Leaving aside the possibility of global variables, the data required by a procedure is provided via the argument sequence, which is enclosed in parentheses, and immediately follows the name of the procedure in the invoking statement. The argument sequence in the next example is k , 2.

```
> show := proc( a , b )

    print( a , b ) :

  end proc :

> k := 3 :
> show( k , 2 ) :
```

$$3, 2$$

Under normal evaluation rules, the arguments are evaluated before being bound to the corresponding entries in the parameter sequence, which is enclosed in parentheses and immediately follows the **proc** keyword. In the above example, the parameter sequence is **a , b**. It is important to consistently and correctly distinguish between the meanings of the terms *argument* and *parameter*. Alliteration provides a good method for recollection: the **p**arameter sequence follows the **p**roc keyword. When the **show** procedure is invoked, the parameters **a** and **b** are replaced by 3 and 2, respectively. Note that a procedure that takes no arguments is permitted, in which case the parameter sequence is empty. Maple also provides facilities for optional arguments, the '*keyword* = *value*' syntax used by some of its own procedures (see Section 6.2 for example), and many other possibilities besides. See Chapter 6 of the Programming Guide (`?ProgrammingGuide,Chapter06`) for full details.

Another feature worthy of a special mention is that procedures can accept the names of other procedures in their argument sequence. The definition of a procedure used as an argument can be accessed using the associated parameter name. For example, suppose we wish to define an operator similar to **D** (see Section 3.7) but for integration. That is,

$$A(g) = \int_0^x g(t)\, dt$$

for any function g, assuming the integral exists. This can be achieved as follows.

```
> A := proc( g )

    local G , t , x :
```

```
   G := int( g( t ) , t = 0 .. x ) :

   return unapply( G , x ) :

  end proc :
> f := x -> x^2 :
> A( f ) ;
```

$$x \rightarrow \frac{1}{3} x^3$$

```
> A( sin )( Pi ) ;
```

$$2$$

Here, the procedure *A* first integrates its argument, and then converts the result from an expression into an operator using **unapply** (returning the expression *G* would create an escaped local). The presence of (Pi) at the end of the last statement causes the result obtained by computing $A(\sin)$ (i.e. $x \rightarrow 1 - \cos(x)$) to be evaluated at the point $x = \pi$, just as it would for D.

It is usually best to think of arguments as input to a procedure, and to use a return statement for output (see Section 8.6). Procedures written in this way do not modify their arguments (this is the most natural approach: one would not expect the value of *x* to change if we ask Maple to compute $\tan x$, for example). Where a procedure needs to modify a parameter value during execution, the usual technique is to copy this into a local variable, so that the value outside the procedure is not affected.

```
> my_proc := proc( x0 )

    local x := x0 :
    #Now do as we please with x, without affecting x0

    statements

  end proc :
```

However, if an argument is an indexed data structure such as an array, then changing the elements from within the procedure is quite common, especially in cases where retaining a copy of the original data is unnecessary. A simple example, in which a procedure assigns a value to every entry in an array, is shown below; the sorting procedure discussed in Section 9.4 uses this feature in a more practical way.

```
> fill_with := proc( A , x )

   local j :

   for j from lowerbound( A ) to upperbound( A ) do
     A[j] := x :
   end do :

   return :

  end proc:
> A := Array( 1 .. 5 ) ;
```

$$[0\,0\,0\,0\,0]$$

```
> fill_with( A , Pi ) :
> A ;
```

$$[\pi\ \pi\ \pi\ \pi\ \pi]$$

The situation becomes more complicated if a procedure needs to alter scalar arguments. Whilst it must be stressed that this is unusual, it is a good exercise in understanding Maple's evaluation rules. Consider the following example.

```
> set_to_zero := proc( a )
    a := 0 :
  end proc :

> b := 7 :
> set_to_zero( b ) ;
Error, (in set_to_zero) illegal use of a formal parameter
> set_to_zero( c ) :
> c ;
```

$$0$$

Naively, it may appear that the first invocation of the procedure sets the value of the variable b to zero, but it is not so. Prior evaluation of b results in the value 7 being bound to a. An error occurs because a subsequently appears on the left-hand side of an assignment. In general, if a parameter is bound to something other than a name, it cannot appear on the left-hand side of an assignment. On the other hand, if a parameter is bound to a name, an assignment to that name from within the procedure is permitted. Before the second invocation of the `set_to_zero` procedure, c has no value, and is therefore unaffected by prior evaluation. In this way, an argument with no assigned value can be used to retrieve output from a procedure.

By default, parameters do not evaluate beyond their binding to the evaluated arguments. Consequently, if an assignment is made to a parameter which is bound to a name then access to that value can only be gained by forcing full evaluation using `eval`. To see this, consider the following.

```
> test := proc( a )

    a := 1 :
    print( a , eval( a ) ) :

    end proc :

> test( b ) ;
```

$$b, 1$$

Here, the name b is bound to the parameter a, which is subsequently assigned the value 1. However, when a is printed it is not evaluated beyond its binding to b, unless `eval` is applied first. In the next example, unevaluation quotes are used to prevent prior evaluation of b. Since a is then bound to a name, it can appear on the left-hand side of an assignment. Its current value can be accessed using `eval`. In this way, the procedure is able to retrieve the existing value of b, and to assign a new value which then persists outside the procedure.

```
> another_test := proc( a )

    print( eval( a ) ) :
    a := 42 :

    return :

    end proc :
```

```
> b := 7 :
> another_test( 'b' ) :
```

7

```
> b ;
```

42

Procedures which automatically block prior evaluation of their arguments can be created using the **evaln** modifier, or the **uneval** modifier. For an argument which is a name, the effect of these is exactly the same: prior evaluation is prevented, so that the corresponding procedure parameter is bound to the name, not to its value. The current value of such a parameter must be obtained using the **eval** command, but assignments can be made in the usual way.

```
> yet_another_test := proc( a :: evaln )

    print( eval( a ) ) :
    a := 42 :

    return :

  end proc :
> b := 7 :
> yet_another_test( b ) :   # No uneval quotes needed.
```

7

```
> b ;
```

42

The difference between the **evaln** and **uneval** modifiers becomes apparent when the argument is not a name. The **uneval** modifier simply blocks all prior evaluation, whereas **evaln** attempts to evaluate the argument to a name and flags an error if this fails. For example, a literal numerical argument can be bound to a parameter with the **uneval** modifier (though of course assignments to this parameter will not then be possible), but **evaln** will not permit this. Execute **?parameter_modifiers** for more details.

8.5 Checking Argument Validity

In most cases, procedures are not executed directly by a human — they are executed automatically by other parts of the worksheet. Therefore it is generally a good idea to check that the input received by a procedure is valid. Without such 'defences', an automated worksheet may continue to run for some time after a problem arises, in which case tracing the source of an eventual error (or incorrect result) can be very difficult and time-consuming. The type operator : : introduced in Section 2.21 can be used for this purpose. For example, suppose that the procedure `my_proc` uses two parameters, *a* and *b*. Both must be numeric values, and *a* must be positive. These restrictions can be enforced as follows.

```
> my_proc := proc( a :: positive , b :: numeric )

    statements

  end proc :
```

With this definition, both of the following statements result in an error.

```
> my_proc( 'Arthur' , 'Pewty' ) :
> my_proc( -1 , 1 ) :
```

If a procedure requires a container structure (vector, matrix, array, etc.) as part of its input, we can test either the type of the argument itself or the type of the argument and the type of its elements. Unlike the situation discussed in Section 2.21, there is no need for unevaluation quotes. For example, if `my_proc` uses a single parameter *A*, which is an array containing real numbers, then the following declaration is appropriate.

```
> my_proc := proc( A :: Array( numeric ) )

    statements

  end proc :
```

Under some circumstances, type checking alone is not sufficient. Conditional statements can be used to perform other tests and, where necessary, the **error** command can be used to display a message and terminate execution. For example, suppose that the procedure `my_proc` requires distinct integers *m* and *n* as its input. Type checking will account for the first condition, and the `error` command is used if *m* = *n*.

```
> my_proc := proc( m :: integer , n :: integer )

    if m = n then
      error "Doesn't work if m = n" :
    end if :

    statements

  end proc :
```

By default, Maple allows procedures to be invoked with more arguments than necessary. There are applications for this, but in most cases it only serves to expose users to potential errors. Consider the next example, which (incorrectly) uses the `double` procedure from the beginning of this chapter.

```
> double := proc( x )

    return 2 * x :

  end proc :
> double( 0,42 * Pi ) ;
```
$$0$$

Here, the invoking statement contains a typographical error: a comma where a decimal point is intended. The effect of this is to pass two arguments, 0 and 42π, to the procedure. The former is bound to the parameter *x* and the latter is ignored. To prevent a procedure from accepting extra arguments, terminate the parameter sequence with a dollar symbol $. With this modification, extraneous arguments cause Maple to flag an error.

```
> double := proc( x , $ )

    return 2 * x :

  end proc :
> double( 0,42 * Pi ) ;
Error, invalid input: too many and/or wrong type of
arguments passed to double; first unused argument is 42*Pi
```

8.6 Data Returned by Procedures

The concept of a return statement, which can be used to set the return value for a procedure, was briefly introduced in Section 8.1. Such a statement has the following general structure.

return *return values* :

Here, *return values* can be a single object or a sequence of objects, or it can be omitted, in which case the procedure returns no result (cf. results returned by statements in Section 2.7). In the examples considered so far, the return statement has always been placed immediately before **end proc**, but this is not necessary. Any number of return statements can occur anywhere in a procedure, and the procedure is terminated if one of these is executed. This is useful for dealing with cases where certain situations should trigger an immediate return, but processing should otherwise continue. The next example shows a procedure that determines whether a particular character c is a member of a string s. It does this by comparing c with the characters of s, one at a time. An immediate return is triggered if a match occurs, and in this case the return value is *true*. Otherwise the process continues until the end of the string is reached. If no match is found, the loop terminates, and the return value is *false*.

```
> contains_char := proc( s :: string , c :: character )

    local r :

    for r in s do

      if r = c then
        return true :
      end if :

    end do :

    return false :   # No match found if we get to here

  end proc :
> contains_char( "abc" , "d" ) ;   # First test
```
$$false$$

```
> contains_char( "abc" , "a" ) ;   # Second test
```
$$true$$

In a case where no return statement is encountered, and execution reaches **end proc**, the return value is the last result computed within the procedure. This feature can easily lead to mistakes, so its use is not recommended. Including a return statement that is not strictly required is harmless, but forgetting one that is necessary may create a procedure that returns incorrect or nonsensical results. The time required to find and eliminate one such error can easily exceed the time needed to type hundreds or even thousands of unnecessary return statements.

8.7 Returning Unevaluated

Under some circumstances, it is useful to allow a procedure to take one or more names as input, and defer processing until values have been assigned to those names. Consider the following.

```
> y := k! ;
```
$$y := k!$$

```
> k := 12 :
> y ;
```
$$479001600$$

Here, k is initially undefined, so the factorial cannot be evaluated when the first statement is executed. However, applying the factorial to a symbol is not an error. It may be possible to evaluate it at a later stage, and indeed, after assigning the value 12 to k, the evaluation occurs at the next instance of the variable y. The key point here is that the factorial is *returned unevaluated* if Maple has insufficient information to compute a result. The next example shows a naive attempt to implement the factorial function using a procedure, and a very common error that occurs when the argument has not been assigned a value.

```
> my_fact := proc( n )

      local f , j :
```

```
f := 1 :

for j from 1 to n do
  f := f * j :
end do :

return f :

end proc :
> my_fact( 7 ) ;

                    5040

> my_fact( p ) ;
Error, (in my_fact) final value in for loop must be numeric
or character
```

In the last statement, the parameter n is bound to the symbol p (which has no value), and the procedure fails when it attempts to set up the loop, because the final value is not a number. We could insist that n should be bound to a nonnegative integer (see Section 8.5), but this would simply change the error message after the last statement. To allow n to be bound to a name or a nonnegative integer, we can delay evaluation as follows.

```
> my_fact := proc( n )

  local f , j :

  if type( n , name ) then
    return 'my_fact( n )' :
  elif not type( n , nonnegint ) then
    error( "Argument must be a name or a
                            nonnegative integer" ) :
  end if :

  f := 1 :

  for j from 1 to n do
    f := f * j :
  end do :

  return f :

end proc :
```

```
> my_fact( 7 ) ;
```

$$5040$$

```
> f := my_fact( p ) ;
```

$$f := my\_fact(p)$$

```
> p := 5 :
> f ;
```

$$120$$

Now, when the statement f := my_fact(p) is executed, the symbol p is bound to the parameter n, and this subsequently causes the conditional statement type(n , name) to evaluate to true. Note that this test also evaluates to *true* if n is bound to an unassigned table entry, whereas type(n , symbol) would evaluate to *false* in such cases. Evaluation of the return value causes the removal of the unevaluation quotes, so that my_fact(p) is the result of the procedure. The next time f appears in a context that causes evaluation, p has the value 5, so my_fact(5) is evaluated.

Many of Maple's own procedures are programmed to accept any input and return unevaluated in any case where a result cannot be computed. This has the advantage that algebraic expressions can be used as arguments; thus (k + 1)! is acceptable input, whereas my_fact(k + 1) would lead to an error in the above example. On the other hand, it has the disadvantage of allowing nonsensical input.

```
> p := plot( x^2 ) :
> p! ;
```

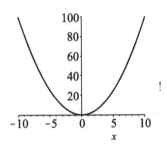

★ A useful shortcut for an unevaluated return from a procedure that has a long name, or that accepts a large number of parameters, is `return 'procname( _passed )'`. The special names `procname` and `_passed` will automatically be replaced by the procedure name and the evaluated argument sequence, respectively.

8.8 Output Displayed from Within Procedures

When a procedure is executed, the results of statements enclosed between `proc( ... )` and `end proc` will be displayed if their nesting level does not exceed the current value of `printlevel` (see Section 7.3). Colons and semicolons inside the procedure body have no bearing on output (cf. conditionals and loops, Sections 7.1 and 7.2, respectively). The nesting level increases by 5 when Maple enters a procedure, and decreases by 5 when the procedure terminates. Since procedures often contain loops and conditionals, and may invoke other procedures, it may be necessary to set `printlevel` to a very large value in order to cause Maple to display the result of a particular statement. Therefore it is usually better to use `print` or `printf` to show the inner workings of a procedure (see Section 7.4). In most cases this is useful for debugging purposes only; once the procedure is working the `print` and `printf` commands are removed or deactivated to prevent unnecessary output, which can slow Maple down significantly.

8.9 Remember Tables and Recursion

A procedure can be made to store the result(s) of each invocation in a *remember table*. The stored results will be used if the procedure is executed again with the same values for its parameters, saving time. To allow a procedure to construct a remember table, simply insert

`option remember :`

somewhere inside the procedure body, before the statement sequence. A remember table can grow to any size, which can cause problems with excessive memory usage. Therefore a *cache table*, obtained by using option `cache` in place of option `remember`, may be preferable. By default, this stores results from the most recent 512 invocations. The number can be changed by using option `cache( N )`, where N is a positive integer.

Cache tables and remember tables are often used with *recursive* procedures, that is, procedures which invoke themselves. The procedure in the next example computes the harmonic numbers

$$S_n = \sum_{j=1}^{n} \frac{1}{n},$$

using the facts that $S_1 = 1$ and

$$S_n = S_{n-1} + \frac{1}{n}, \quad n \geq 2.$$

For example, S_3 is computed as

$$S_3 = \frac{1}{3} + S_2$$
$$= \frac{1}{3} + \frac{1}{2} + S_1$$
$$= \frac{1}{3} + \frac{1}{2} + 1$$
$$= \frac{11}{6}.$$

Computing S_3 causes S_3, S_2 and S_1 to be added to the remember table. Increasing `printlevel` (see Section 8.8) and calling the procedure again with $n = 4$ shows that Maple has indeed remembered the value of S_3, and uses this to compute S_4 in a single step.

```
> harmonic_number := proc( n :: posint )

    option remember :

    if n = 1 then
      return 1 :
    else
      return harmonic_number( n - 1 ) + 1 / n :
    end if :

  end proc :
```

```
> harmonic_number( 3 ) ;
```

$$\frac{11}{6}$$

```
> printlevel := 20 :
> harmonic_number( 4 ) ;
{--> enter harmonic_number, args = 4
value remembered (in harmonic_number): harmonic_number(3)
-> 11/6
<-- exit harmonic_number (now at top level) = 25/12}
```

$$\frac{25}{12}$$

★ It is possible to insert an entry into a procedure's remember table by making an assignment to a function call.

```
> harmonic_number( 10 ) := 7381 / 2520 :
```

However, this is not recommended, because it changes the behaviour of the procedure from outside its definition.

★ Some of Maple's own commands use remember tables; these include diff, evalf, expand, normal and series.

★ The time command can be used to assess the performance of Maple code. Obviously timing will produce different results on different machines, but one must also be wary of remember tables when using this facility.

```
> time( evalf[ 100000 ]( Pi ) ) ;
```

$$0.295$$

```
> time( evalf[ 100000 ]( Pi ) ) ;
```

$$0.$$

8.10 Viewing a Procedure Definition

Procedures use last name evaluation, which means that a procedure name evaluates to itself. This is the reason why eval was needed in Section 3.4 to reveal that the name tan is associated with a procedure.

verboseproc value	0	1	2	3
Maple library procedure	PS	PS	FD	FDRT
User-defined procedure	PS	FD	FD	FDRT

Table 8.1 *Output produced by applying* **eval** *to a procedure name. Key: PS –*
parameter sequence, FD – full definition, FDRT – full definition and remember
table. The default value of **verboseproc** *is* 1.

```
> whattype( tan ) ;
```

symbol

```
> whattype( eval( tan ) ) ;
```

procedure

Forcing a full evaluation using **eval** is a useful way to obtain information
about procedures whose definition is not located in the current worksheet.
This could be a user-defined procedure stored in a library (execute
?LibraryTools for details), or one of Maple's own procedures. Exactly
what is displayed depends on the **verboseproc** interface variable. The
effects of **eval** at different values are shown in Table 8.1 There is one
caveat concerning Maple's own procedures. The core part of Maple
(called the *kernel*) is implemented in C. Procedures that form part
of the kernel are said to be *built-in*, and their definitions cannot be
viewed. However, most commands are part of the *Maple library*, which
is implemented in the Maple language itself. Full definitions of library
commands can be viewed using **eval**.

```
> interface( verboseproc = 2 ) :
> eval( seq ) ;   # seq is a kernel command
```

proc( ) **option** *builtin = seq;* **end proc**

```
> interface( verboseproc = 2 ) :
> eval( tan ) ;   # tan is a library command.
                  # This generates a lot of output.
```

An alternative method is to use the **showstat** command, which is not
affected by **verboseproc**. However, **showstat** omits options and will
generate a lot of additional output if **printlevel** is set to a high value.
Applying **showstat** to a kernel command results in an error.

```
> showstat( seq ) ;
Error, (in showstat) cannot debug built-in functions
> showstat( tan ) ;   # This generates a lot of output
> printlevel := 20 :
> showstat( tan ) ;   # This generates even more output
```

The **showstat** command has some additional features to assist with debugging; execute **?showstat** for details.

9

Example Programs

We end this book with some examples that bring together many of the ideas introduced. In each case, a brief analysis of a problem is presented along with a Maple procedure to solve it, and some annotations to explain the thinking that went into each part of the code.

9.1 Pascal's Triangle

Pascal's triangle contains the binomial coefficients

$$C_j^n = \binom{n}{j} = \frac{n!}{j!(n-j)!}, \quad n = 0, 1, \ldots \quad j = 0, 1, \ldots n.$$

Here, n is the row number and j is the column number. The first few rows are shown below.

```
          1
         1  1
        1  2  1
       1  3  3  1
      1  4  6  4  1
     1  5  10  10  5  1
```

Evidently, if $j = 0$ or $j = n$ then $C_j^n = 1$. Elsewhere, the entries may be obtained from those in the preceding row using the relationship

$$C_j^n = C_j^{n-1} + C_{j-1}^{n-1},$$

which requires far less work than using the binomial formula directly. Program 9.1 shows a procedure that uses this to generate the first $N + 1$ rows of Pascal's triangle. Let us examine how this works.

1 & 17 The beginning and end of the procedure definition are marked

200

by **proc** and **end proc**, respectively. We give the procedure a sensible name, and insist that N (the last row in which coefficients are to be calculated) must be a nonnegative integer.

2–3 The description is particularly important here because an unwary user could easily commit an off-by-one error by failing to realise that the rows are numbered from zero.

4 The local variables n and j will be used as loop indices for the row and column numbers, respectively.

5 Since the shape of the data is not rectangular, a table is the most natural choice of container in which to store the results. Using an ordinary array or matrix here would lead to a large amount of redundant storage, though one might consider a sparse matrix or sparse array (only the nonzero entries in a sparse structure are stored; execute **?sparse** for details).

6 & 15 The outer do loop; the index n loops over rows 0 to N of the triangle.

7 & 14 The inner do loop; the index j loops over columns 0 to n in row n.

8–13 Entries on the left and right edges are all given by $C_0^n = C_n^n = 1$. Elsewhere, the recurrence relation is used.

16 The **eval** command is applied to the return value, to prevent the appearance of an escaped local variable (see Section 8.3).

Note the use of the **seq** command introduced in Section 2.20 in testing the procedure by displaying rows of results; it is not possible to retrieve a sequence of values from a table using the range operator.

```
1  > Pascal := proc( N :: nonnegint )

2      description "Generates rows 0 .. N of Pascal's
3                                          triangle" :
4      local n , j :
5      local C := table() :

6      for n from 0 to N do  # n is the row number
7        for j from 0 to n do  # j is the column number

8          if j = 0 or j = n then
9            C[j,n] := 1 :
10         else
11           # Recurrence relation
12           C[j,n] := C[j,n-1] + C[j-1,n-1] :
13         end if :

14       end do :
15     end do :

16     return eval( C ) :

17   end proc :
   > # Test
   > C := Pascal( 8 ) :
   > seq( C[j,4] , j = 0 .. 4 ) ;
                            1, 4, 6, 4, 1

   > seq( C[j,8] , j = 0 .. 8 ) ;
                        1, 8, 28, 56, 70, 56, 28, 8, 1
```

Program 9.1 A procedure for generating Pascal's triangle.

9.2 The Collatz Problem

For a given initial value n_0, the sequence defined by

$$n_{j+1} = \begin{cases} \dfrac{n_j}{2} & \text{if } n \text{ is even,} \\ 3n_j + 1 & \text{if } n \text{ is odd,} \end{cases}$$

may eventually settle into the cycle 1, 4, 2, 1, 4, 2, . . . Determining whether this happens for every $n_0 \in \mathbb{N}$ is known as the *Collatz problem*, which remains unsolved at the time of writing. Program 9.2 shows a procedure that tests the outcome for a given initial value and number of iterations. Let us examine how this works.

1–2 & 21 The beginning and end of the procedure definition are marked by **proc** and **end proc**, respectively. We give the procedure a sensible name, and insist that the initial value is a positive integer. Users of the procedure are able to set the maximum number of iterations to try, and to decide whether to display the values obtained at each step.

3–4 A brief description explaining the purpose of the procedure.

5 The initial value n_0 is copied into a local variable n, which can subsequently be changed (see Section 8.4).

6 A local variable j is declared for use as the step number.

7 & 19 The do loop. Since we don't know a priori that the iteration will enter the cycle, a limit is imposed on the number of steps.

8–12 The conditional statement determines whether n is currently odd or even, using the **mod** command (execute ?mod for more details). The value is then updated to the next member of the sequence.

13–15 The step number and the value of n in the current step are displayed, if *display* evaluates to *true*.

16–18 If the cycle has been entered, the procedure terminates, and returns *true* as its result.

20 This line is reached only if the loop ends without the sequence entering the cycle 1, 4, 2, 1, 4, 2, . . . Therefore *false* is returned as the result in this case.

```
1  > Collatz := proc( n0 :: posint , max_its :: posint ,
2                                      display :: boolean )

3      description "Tests the Collatz problem with initial
4                                           value n0" :

5      local n := n0 :
6      local j :

7      for j from 1 to max_its do

8        if n mod 2 = 0 then
9          n := n / 2 :
10       else
11         n := 3 * n + 1 :
12       end if :

13       if display then
14         printf( "%8d %8d\n" , j , n ) :
15       end if :

16       if n = 1 or n = 2 or n = 4 then
17         return true :
18       end if :

19     end do :

20     return false :

21   end proc :
   > Collatz( 10 , 100000 , true ) :  # Test 1
         1       5
         2      16
         3       8
         4       4
   > Collatz( 999999 , 100000 , false ) ;  # Test 2
                        true
```

Program 9.2 A demonstration of the Collatz problem.

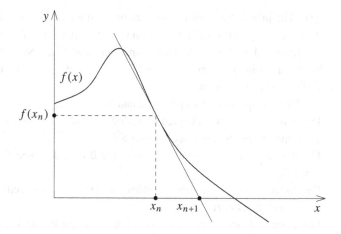

Figure 9.1 Schematic diagram illustrating one step of the Newton–Raphson iteration.

9.3 A Newton–Raphson Iteration

Suppose that x_n is close to a root of the function f. The point at which the tangent to the graph of $f(x)$ at $x = x_n$ intercepts the x axis is often closer to the root than x_n itself (see Figure 9.1). Since this tangent is a straight line through the point $(x_n, f(x_n))$, its equation is

$$y = (x - x_n)f'(x_n) + f(x_n).$$

Setting $y = 0$ and $x = x_{n+1}$ (the new estimate), we obtain the Newton–Raphson iteration formula

$$x_{n+1} = x_n - \frac{f(x_n)}{f'(x_n)},$$

which is widely used to home in on solutions to nonlinear equations. Program 9.3 shows a procedure that can be used to apply this method to an arbitrary function. The purpose of each line is described below.

1-2 & 15 The beginning and end of the procedure definition are marked by **proc** and **end proc**, respectively. We give the procedure a sensible name, and insist that each argument has the correct type. The procedure requires an operator f, an initial estimate for the root x_0 (which must be a number), a maximum number of iterations and a tolerance ϵ. There is no guarantee that a Newton–Raphson iteration will converge, but the procedure will terminate if $|f(x)| < \epsilon$ at any step.

3-4 A brief description of the procedure and its purpose.

5 The initial estimate x_0 is copied into a local variable x, which can subsequently be changed (see Section 8.4).

6 The derivative of f is obtained, using the D operator (see Section 3.7).

7 & 13 The do loop allows for a limited number of iterations, as specified by the parameter *max_its*.

8 The comment here serves as a reminder that the iteration can generate very large expressions if it feeds exact results back into the formula.

9 The iteration formula is used to update x.

10-12 An immediate return is triggered if $|f(x)| < \epsilon$. In this case, the procedure returns the final value of x followed by *true*, to indicate that the iteration has achieved the required tolerance.

14 This line is reached only if the do loop terminates having performed the maximum allowed number of iterations without achieving the required condition $|f(x)| < \epsilon$. Therefore the final value of x is now followed by *false*.

Note the small number of steps used in testing the procedure; when a Newton–Raphson iteration converges it usually does so very rapidly.

```
1   > Newton_Raphson := proc( f :: operator , x0 :: numeric ,
2                       max_its :: posint , epsilon :: positive )

3       description "Applies the Newton-Raphson formula to
4                           f( x ), using the initial value x0" :

5       local x  := x0 :      # Initial guess
6       local df := D( f ) :  # Obtain derivative

7       from 1 to max_its do

8         #Don't forget evalf when using Newton-Raphson
9         x := evalf( x - f( x ) / df( x ) ) :

10        if ( abs( f( x ) ) < epsilon ) then
11           return x , true :
12        end if

13      end do :

14      return x , false :

15    end proc :

    > f := x -> x^2 - 2 :  # Test 1
    > r := Newton_Raphson( f , 1.5 , 3 , 10^(-8) ) ;
```

$$r := 1.414213562, true$$

```
    > f( r[1] ) ;
```

$$-1.\, 10^{-9}$$

```
    > g := x -> sin( x ) * exp( x ) - 2 * x :  # Test 2
    > r := Newton_Raphson( g , 1 , 5 , 10^(-8) ) ;
```

$$0.8030341928, true$$

```
    > g( r[1] ) ;
```

$$0.$$

Program 9.3 A Newton–Raphson procedure.

9.4 Sorting Data

A common programming task is to sort an array containing numerical data into ascending order. There are many algorithms that can be used for sorting. We will use a *selection sort*, which works by finding the smallest array element, and swapping it with the first. Next it finds the second smallest element, and swaps this with the second element, etc. Suppose we start with an array containing the five elements 1, 3, −2, 7 and −3 (in this order). For this small example, the algorithm is represented diagrammatically in Figure 9.2. In locating the correct entry for position j, any preceding elements can be ignored, because these have already been positioned correctly by earlier steps. After four steps, four elements are positioned correctly, so the last element has been automatically moved into the correct position because there is nowhere else for it to go. An implementation for an array of arbitrary size is given in Program 9.4. The purpose of each line is described below.

1 & 19 The beginning and end of the procedure definition are marked by **proc** and **end proc**, respectively. We give the procedure a sensible name, and insist that the input consists of an array containing numerical values.

2–3 A brief description explaining the purpose of the procedure.

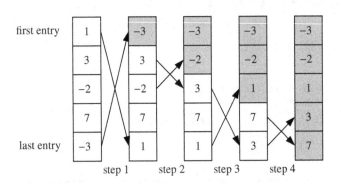

Figure 9.2 Sorting an array into ascending order by selection. Shaded areas show where elements have been positioned correctly by preceding steps.

4–5 Local variable declarations.

7–9 We check for a potential problem with the input: the array must be one-dimensional, or the sorting algorithm will not work.

10–11 The bounds for the array index are stored for later use.

12 & 17 The do loop. The index j refers to the position at which the entry is to be corrected during the current step. Thus, the smallest element is placed into the first position on the first step, etc. The loop stops one step before the end of the array. As noted above, if all but one of the elements have been swapped into place then the last element must also be in the correct position.

13 This comment explains the purpose of line 14, which may not be immediately apparent.

14 The **min** command with the **index** option locates the smallest element that currently resides in position j or later. This (along with a corresponding option for **max**) was introduced in Maple 2015; in earlier versions another loop would be needed to perform the search.

15 The syntax by which Maple allows variables to be swapped in a single step is not widely known, so an explanatory comment is included.

16 The current element (j) is swapped with the smallest element in position j or later (m). This has no effect if j and m have the same value.

18 The **return** statement. The effect of this procedure is to rearrange the entries of A, so there is no return value.

```
1   > sort_ascending := proc( A :: Array( numeric ) )

2       description "Uses a selection sort to put the entries
3                                 of A into ascending order." :

4       local lb , ub :
5       local j , m :

6       # Check number of dimensions
7       if ArrayNumDims( A ) <> 1 then
8         error "Only 1D arrays can be sorted." :
9       end if :

10      lb := lowerbound( A ) :
11      ub := upperbound( A ) :

12      for j from lb to ub - 1 do

13        # Find the smallest element in position j or later
14        m := min[ index ]( A[j..] ) :  # Maple 2015 & later

15        # Swap elements into position
16        A[j] , A[m] := A[m] , A[j] :

17      end do :

18      return :

19    end proc :

    > # Test
    > A := Array( [ 2 , -1 , 7 , 23 , 3 , 1 , 0 , -10 ] ) :
    > sort_ascending( A ) ;
    > A ;
```

$$[-10, -1, 0, 1, 2, 3, 7, 23]$$

Program 9.4 A selection sort procedure.

9.5 Quadrature Formulae

If $|b - a|$ is small, we might approximate the integral

$$I = \int_a^b f(x)\,dx$$

using the area of the trapezium with vertices

$$(a, 0), \quad (a, f(a)), \quad (b, 0) \quad \text{and} \quad (b, f(b))$$

(see Figure 9.3). This gives us the trapezium rule

$$I \approx \frac{b - a}{2}[f(a) + f(b)].$$

A more accurate approximation is Simpson's rule, which uses $f(a)$ and $f(b)$ alongside the value of the function f at the centre of the integration range; thus

$$I \approx \frac{b - a}{6}\left[f(a) + 4f\left(\frac{b + a}{2}\right) + f(b)\right].$$

In general, if we write

$$x_j = a + j\Delta x \quad \text{with} \quad \Delta x = \frac{b - a}{N},$$

these approximations (which are called Newton–Cotes quadrature rules) have the form

$$I \approx (b - a)[w_0 f(x_0) + w_1 f(x_1) + \cdots + w_N f(x_N)].$$

Note that $x_0 = a$ and $x_N = b$. Since the index starts from 0, there are $N + 1$ nodes x_j and $N + 1$ *weights* w_j. One way to find the weights is to demand that the result should be exact if $f(x) = x^p$, for $p = 0, 1, \ldots, N$. It turns out that the end-points a and b can be chosen arbitrarily (provided $b \neq a$). We will take $a = 0$ and $b = 1$ to obtain a result of the form

$$\int_0^1 f(x)\,dx \approx [w_0 f(x_0) + w_1 f(x_1) + \cdots + w_N f(x_N)],$$

where now $x_j = j/N$, but we can return to the integral over $[a, b]$ by writing

$$f(x) = g(a + (b - a)x)$$

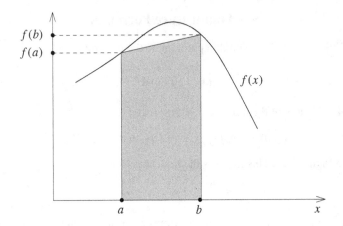

Figure 9.3 Schematic diagram showing the approximation used by the trapezium rule.

and then making the substitution $t = a + (b - a)x$. None of this affects the values of the weights w_j. Now, if $f(x) = x^p$, then

$$\int_0^1 x^p \, \mathrm{d}x = \frac{1}{p+1},$$

so we must have

$$\frac{1}{p+1} = w_0 x_0^p + w_1 x_1^p + \cdots + w_N x_N^p \quad \text{for} \quad p = 0, 1, \ldots, N. \quad (*)$$

The trapezium rule uses two nodes, so $N = 1$, and it should give an exact result if $f(x) = x^0 \equiv 1$, or $f(x) = x$. Setting $p = 0$ in $(*)$, we find that

$$1 = w_0 + w_1,$$

and then with $p = 1$ we obtain

$$\frac{1}{2} = w_1,$$

so that $w_0 = 1/2$ as well. We can obtain Simpson's rule in the same way, setting $N = 2$ so that there are three weights w_0, w_1 and w_2, and requiring exact results for $f(x) \equiv 1$, $f(x) = x$ and $f(x) = x^2$, corresponding to the cases where $p = 0$, 1 and 2, respectively. However, doing this manually becomes very tedious as the number of nodes is increased. Program 9.5 automates the process. Let us examine how this works.

1 & 17   The beginning and end of the procedure definition are marked by **proc** and **end proc**, respectively. We give the procedure a sensible name, and insist that N is a nonnegative integer.

2-3   A brief description explaining the purpose of the procedure, noting that it computes weights for $N + 1$ point quadrature (which is why $N = 0$ is permitted). As in the case of Pascal's triangle (Section 9.1), the description helps users avoid a potential off-by-one error.

4-6   Local variable declarations. Capital letters are used for the variables **LHS** and **RHS**, to avoid confusion with the **lhs** and **rhs** commands.

7   A table for storing the weights w_j is assigned. We need to form a system of equations and solve for these values, and we will take advantage of the fact that unassigned table entries can be treated like ordinary variables (see Section 7.6).

8   An array for storing the equations is assigned.

9 & 13   This do loop forms the equations to be solved. Each iteration generates one equation, with the index p corresponding to the power in x^p. Ultimately, the loop creates $N + 1$ equations for the $N + 1$ unknowns, because p ranges from 0 to N.

10   The left-hand side of equation p from (*) is stored.

11   The right-hand side of equation p is constructed using **add**.

12   Equation p is stored.

14   A set of variables is formed. Recall that the **solve** command solves a set of equations for a set of unknowns (see Section 4.2).

15   The array containing the equations is converted into a set before being passed to the **solve** command. Note the use of **assign** (see Section 4.2) to convert the solutions into assignments so that they are stored for later use.

16   The weights are returned in a list.

```
1   > NC_weights := proc( N :: nonnegint )

2       description "Computes weights for N + 1 point
3                                   Newton-Cotes quadrature" :

4       local p , j :
5       local LHS , RHS :
6       local w , eqns , vars :

7       w    := table() :
8       eqns := Array( 0 .. N ) :

9       for p from 0 to N do

10          LHS := 1 / ( p + 1 ) :
11          RHS := add( w[j] * ( j / N )^p , j = 0 .. N ) :

12          eqns[p] := LHS = RHS :  # Store equations

13      end do :

14      vars := { seq( w[p] , p = 0 .. N ) } :

15      assign( solve( convert( eqns , set ) , vars ) ) :

16      return [ seq( w[p] , p = 0 .. N ) ] :

17  end proc :
    > # Test
    > NC_weights( 2 ) ;
```

$$\left[\frac{1}{6}, \frac{2}{3}, \frac{1}{6}\right]$$

```
    > NC_weights( 5 ) ;
```

$$\left[\frac{19}{288}, \frac{25}{96}, \frac{25}{144}, \frac{25}{144}, \frac{25}{96}, \frac{19}{288}\right]$$

Program 9.5 Derivation of Newton–Cotes quadrature rules.

9.6 Necklaces

Suppose that a necklace is to be made from n beads, each of which can be either black or white. We wish to determine how many distinct designs are possible. The answer isn't 2^n (i.e. two colour choices in each of the n positions), because many of the arrangements can be obtained from others by rotation. We need to find a way to eliminate these duplicate designs, and since 2^n grows very rapidly with n, our method will need to be very efficient. The key observation to make is that a unique integer value can be assigned to each arrangement by cutting the necklace, putting the beads in a straight line, and treating this as a binary sequence, taking black and white beads to represent 1 and 0, respectively. An example is shown in Figure 9.4. Rotating the necklace can be simulated by moving the digit from the left end of the sequence to the right end. For the 8-bit sequence in Figure 9.4, this would mean subtracting 128 to remove the leftmost digit, multiplying by 2 to shift the remaining digits to the left, and adding 1 to set the rightmost bit to 1. Hence, the result of rotating by one place is

$$2(177 - 128) + 1 = 99 = 2^6 + 2^5 + 2^1 + 2^0.$$

Since the leftmost bit is now set to 0, another rotation can be performed by simply doubling, which shifts each digit to the left and introduces a trailing zero.

Now consider the general case, in which an integer j is represented by an n-bit binary sequence. The highest possible value for j is $2^n - 1$, and the lowest is 0. The value of the leftmost bit is 2^{n-1}, so if $j < 2^{n-1}$ then the sequence must begin with a zero. After discarding this, multiplying by 2 shifts the remaining digits left one place, and introduces a trailing zero in the rightmost position. On the other hand, if $j \geq 2^{n-1}$, then the leftmost bit must first be removed by subtracting 2^{n-1}. The resulting value must then be doubled to shift left and finally increased by 1 to change the rightmost bit to 1. Our rotation operator is therefore given by

$$r(j) = \begin{cases} 2j & \text{if } j < 2^{n-1}, \\ 2(j - 2^{n-1}) + 1 & \text{otherwise.} \end{cases}$$

Since the value of 2^{n-1} is fixed for each n, a rotation requires one

Figure 9.4 Representation of a necklace by a binary sequence. In this case
the value of the sequence is $2^7 + 2^5 + 2^4 + 2^0 = 128 + 32 + 16 + 1 = 177$.

conditional statement and two arithmetic operations on average. Clearly,
n rotations will return the starting value, but fewer rotations will achieve
this in some cases (for example $r(0) = 0$ and $r(2^n - 1) = 2^n - 1$; these
correspond to the case in which all of the beads are white, and the case in
which all of the beads are black, respectively). A procedure that computes
the number of possible necklaces for a given n is shown in Program 9.6.
Let us examine how this works.

1 & 27 The beginning and end of the procedure definition are marked
by **proc** and **end proc**, respectively. We give the procedure a
sensible name, and insist that the number of beads n is a positive
integer.

2–3 A brief description of the procedure and its purpose.

4 The local variable ud will be used to count the number of unique
designs found. It is initially set to zero.

5 The value of the leftmost bit in the binary sequence, 2^{n-1}, is stored
to avoid repeated computation.

6 An array with its entries initially set to *true* is created. The index
ranges from 0 to $2^n - 1$. If we find that the binary representation of
j corresponds to a necklace design that has already been counted,
then A_j will be set to *false*.

7 The local variable j will be used as a loop index. The local variable
c will be used to store values obtained by repeatedly applying the
rotation operation r, starting with the initial value j.

8 & 25 The outer do loop. The index j ranges over all valid indices in the
array A.

9–11 If A_j has already been set to *false*, then j, and all values that can
be obtained by repeatedly applying the rotation operation starting

from j, have been discounted. Therefore we move immediately to the next step in the outer loop.

12 If this point is reached, then a unique necklace design has been found. The counter is updated.

13 The current value of the index j is copied into another local variable, c.

14 & 24 The inner do loop. A new value for c is obtained at each step by applying the rotation operator r to the old value. After n steps, we will always return to the original value, but this may happen sooner, so a loop with a break statement and no limits is appropriate.

15–19 The value of c is updated by applying the rotation operator.

20–22 If c has returned to its original value (j), then all possible values that can be obtained by rotation have been discarded, and nothing can be gained by further iterations. The inner do loop is then terminated by the break statement.

23 If c has not returned to its original value, then the design corresponding to c is a rotation of the design corresponding to j. Therefore A_c is set to *false*.

26 The number of unique designs is returned as the result of the procedure.

Even for a modern computer, the demands of this procedure are very high, and using a large value for n may cause Maple to freeze.

```
1  > necklace_number := proc( n :: posint )

2       description "Finds the number of distinct necklaces
3           with n beads; each bead is either black or white." :

4       local ud  := 0 :
5       local lbv := 2^(n-1) :  # left bit value
6       local A   := Array( 0 .. 2^n - 1 , fill = true ) :
7       local j , c :

8       for j from 0 to upperbound( A ) do

9         if not A[j] then
10          next :
11        end if :

12        ud := ud + 1 :
13        c  := j :

14        do
15          if c < lbv then
16            c := 2 * c :
17          else
18            c := 2 * ( c - lbv ) + 1 :
19          end if :

20          if c = j then
21            break :
22          end if :

23          A[c] := false :

24        end do :
25      end do :

26      return ud :

27    end proc :

   > necklace_number( 2 ) , necklace_number( 18 ) ;  # Tests
                         3, 14602
```

Program 9.6 Counting necklace designs.

Appendix A

Other Ways to Run Maple

Command line Maple is useful for batch processing, and places less demand on system resources than the Standard Worksheet Interface. It has limited features for displaying results, but exactly the same processing power as the full version. To access command line Maple conveniently, it is generally best to update the PATH environment variable so that the system command interpreter can find the executable file. This is called maple (with a lower case 'm') on unix systems (including Macs) and cmaple.exe on Windows. The exact procedure for changing PATH varies from one platform to another; contact your system administrator for assistance. Once the PATH environment variable has been set, command line Maple can be started by entering maple (cmaple on Windows) at the system command prompt, which is represented by the symbol % in the following examples.

```
% maple
    |\^/|     Maple 2016 (APPLE UNIVERSAL OSX)
._|\|   |/|_. Copyright (c) Maplesoft, a division of ...
 \  MAPLE  /  All rights reserved. Maple is a trademark of
 <____ ____>  Waterloo Maple Inc.
      |       Type ? for help.
> expand( ( x + 1 )^2 ) ;
                            2
                           x  + 2 x + 1
> evalf( BesselJ( 1 , 2.5 ) ) ;
                           0.4970941025
> quit ;
memory used=0.6MB, alloc=8.3MB, time=0.04
%
```

Note the quit command, which is used to terminate command line Maple (this is disabled in the Standard Worksheet Interface). Previous commands (including those from earlier sessions) can be retrieved using the cursor up arrow key, after which they can be edited and executed again. There is no concept of an execution group in command line Maple, and holding ⸢shift⸣ does not change the effect of pressing ⸢return⸣. Instead, input that is not terminated by a colon or semicolon is assumed to continue on the next line. The next example would cause an error in the Standard Worksheet Interface.

```
> x := 2 ; y :=
                         x := 2
> 5 ;
                         y := 5
```

The **read** command is often used to cause command line Maple to read statements from a plain text file (not a worksheet!). Files used for this purpose are usually given the extension .mpl. By default, statements read in are not displayed, but this can be changed by using the **interface** command to set the **echo** interface variable to 2, 3 or 4. The next two examples assume that the file **test.mpl** contains the following statements.

```
simplify( sin( x )^2 + cos( x )^2 ) ;
print( "That was easy" ) ;
```

```
> read( "test.mpl" ) ;
                         1

                   "That was easy"
> interface( echo = 2 ) :
> read( "test.mpl" ) ;
> simplify( sin( x )^2 + cos( x )^2 ) ;
                         1
> print( "That was easy" ) ;
                   "That was easy"
```

It is also possible to read an mpl file directly from the system command line. In this case, the commands read will be displayed unless Maple is started with the −q (quiet) option.

```
% maple -q test.mpl
                         1

                   "That was easy"
```

The **save** command is a partial analogue to **read**. It can be used to store variables and procedure definitions in a plain text file.

```
> a := 13 :
> f := proc( x )
>    return x^3 :
> end proc :
> save( a , f , "test2.mpl" ) :
> unassign( 'a' , 'f' ) :
> a , f( -2 ) ;
                            a, f(-2)
> read( "test2.mpl" ) :
> a , f( -2 ) ;
                            13, -8
```

Of course these facilities are also available in the Standard Worksheet Interface, but the **LibraryTools** package offers more sophisticated facilities for storing and reusing code. Another command that is frequently used with command line Maple is **fprintf**, which is similar to **printf** (see Section 7.4), but sends output to a file. The file must be opened using **fopen**, and it's best to close it using **fclose** when it is no longer needed, because data may not be written to the disk until this happens. Maple automatically closes files upon exit, but data that has not been written to the disk may be lost if the session terminates unexpectedly. In the next example, the file `results.txt` is associated with the name *F*. Subsequently, **fprintf** is used to write the approximate value of π into this file. Because the second argument to **fopen** is WRITE, any existing file `results.txt` in the current directory will be overwritten. Alternatively, APPEND can be used, in which case new material is added to the end of an existing file.

```
> F := fopen( "results.txt" , WRITE ) :
> fprintf( F , "%15.10f" , Pi ) :
> fclose( F ) :
```

Execute **?maple** for more information about command line Maple.

It is also possible for other software to interact directly with the Maple engine. This is achieved using OpenMaple, which provides application programmer interfaces (APIs) for C, C#, Java and Visual Basic. A program written in one of these languages can use OpenMaple to execute Maple commands and retrieve results. Example programs can be found in the `samples` folder, which is part of a standard Maple installation. Execute `?OpenMaple` for full details of OpenMaple.

Appendix B

Terminating Characters

Many of the examples in this book include terminating characters — meaning colons or semicolons — in locations where they are optional. This helps to keep things simple: including a terminating character when it is not needed is harmless, but omitting one that is needed will cause a syntax error or worse. Nevertheless, some users may be keen to save typing, so let us now summarise the rules concerning terminating characters.

- Where a terminating character is optional, omitting it is equivalent to using a semicolon.
- Help requests using the ? operator do not need a terminating character.
- In the Standard Worksheet Interface for Maple 2015 and later, statements at the top level (i.e. outside any procedures, loops and conditional statements) do not need a terminating character, unless followed by a comment or another statement in the same execution group.

```
> 2 + 2
```

$$4$$

```
> 2 + 2  # Semicolon needed before hash symbol
>
Warning, premature end of input, use <Shift> + <Enter>
to avoid this message.
> 2 + 2
  3 + 3
Error, unexpected number
```

- In the Standard Worksheet Interface for Maple 18 and earlier, top level statements generate warnings unless they have terminating characters.

```
> 2 + 2
Warning, inserted missing semicolon at end of statement
```

$$4$$

- In command line Maple (all versions), a top level statement that is not a help request will not be processed until it has been terminated with a colon or a semicolon (see Appendix A).
- Inside a procedure, do loop or conditional statement, all statements need terminating characters, except those immediately preceding **end proc**, **elif**, **else**, **end if** or **end do** (or the abbreviations **end**, **fi** or **od**). A comment is permitted to follow such a statement, even if the terminating character is omitted (cf. top level statements, above). However, omitting the terminating characters in these cases can lead to syntax errors when statements are rearranged, so it is not recommended.

```
> a := 1 :
> if a > 0 then

    print( "Hello" )    :  # (semi)colon needed
    print( "Goodbye" )     # (semi)colon not needed

  end if :
```
$$\text{"Hello"}$$
$$\text{"Goodbye"}$$

Similar rules apply to some other structures not discussed in this book (such as modules).

Index of Maple Notation

! 13
" 34
17
$ (sequence operator) 92
$ (for terminating parameter
    sequences) 190
% (ditto operator) 14
% (in format strings) 160–161
%% 14–15
%%% 14–15
&x 125–126
' 37–39, 41
( ) (for grouping) 12
( ) (for command arguments) 12
( ) (for indices) 121, 166–167
* 13
(* *) 17
** 16, 25
+ 13
, 48
- 13
-> 81–86
. (decimal point) 21
. (for noncommutative
    multiplication) 124–125
.. 55, 58–59
/ 13
: 19–20, 148, 150, 158, 223–224
:- 65
:: 64, 188–189
:= 31
; (for terminating matrix rows) 118
; (for terminating statements) 10–11, 21,
    148, 150, 158, 223–224
< (relational operator) 44–48
<= 44–48
<> (relational operator) 44–48

< > (delimiters) 117–118
= 31–32, 44–48
> (prompt symbol) 10, 18
> (relational operator) 44–48
>= 44–48
? 9–10
[ ] (for creating lists) 51
[ ] (for indices) 53–56, 120–122, 164–168
\n 160–161
^ 13, 25, 74
_passed 195
` 35
{ } 49–51
| 117–118
|| 43–44
~ 56–58

about 100
abs 25, 28
add 60–62, 90, 170
aleph 35
algsubs 79
allvalues 108
alpha 35
anames 36
and 46, 83, 99, 149
animate 144–146
APPEND 221
arccos 25
arccosh 25
arcsin 25
arcsinh 25
arctan 25–26
arctanh 25
argument 28
array 163
Array (command) 163
Array (option) 163

225

ArrayNumDims 210
assign 107–108
assume 99–102
assuming 75, 99
axiscoordinates 138

BesselJ 139
beta 48
black 135
blue 136
break 153–155
by 152–153

cat 42–44
coeff 76–77
collect 76–77
color 136
colour 135
complex (option) 72, 109
complex (type) 63
conjugate 28
constrained 137
contour 143–144
contourplot 139, 144
contours 139
convert 28, 75, 97, 119, 141, 163
coords 137–138
copy 130–132, 167, 173
cos 25
cosh 25
CrossProduct 125

D 92–93, 114–115
dash 135
dataplot 141–144
DefiniteSum 89
denom 77–78
Describe 32–33, 170, 177
description 177
Determinant 127
Diff 92
diff 92–93, 197
Digits 23
discont 106, 136
display 140–143, 145–146
do 150–158
DotProduct 125
dsolve 103, 113–116

echo 220
Eigenvalues 128
Eigenvectors 128
elif 149–150
else 149–150
end 147, 150, 174
end do 150
end if 147–148
end proc 174–175, 192
entries 170
EqualEntries 131
error 190
eval 40–42, 80, 170, 181–183, 187–188, 197–198
evalb 45–48, 64, 100
evalc 29
evalf 22–23, 197
evalhf 24
evaln (command) 42
evaln (modifier) 188
exp (command) 25–27, 30
exp (option) 30
expand 72–73, 197
expanded 75
explicit 105, 108
external_calling 70

factor 71–72
fclose 221
fi 147
fibonacci 66
fill 118, 163
filledregions 106, 139
fopen 221
for 151–158
fprintf 221
frac 149
frames 145
from 150–157
frontend 73
fsolve 103, 109–113

Gamma 35
gamma 22
global 179–180
green 136

harmonic 174

HFloat 24
I 27–28, 30
if 147–150
ifactor 155
Im 28
imaginaryunit 30
in 52, 59–60, 157
index 209, 210
indices 170
infinity 87, 89, 94
Int 94–96
int 94–96
integer 62
interface 30, 102, 122–123, 198, 220
intersect 50
is 47–48, 100
isprime 155, 158

kernelopts 23–24

labels 134, 136
legend 136
lhs 44–45
Limit 88
limit 87–88
line 138
Linear 107
LinearSolve 129
linestyle 135, 138
list 63, 119
listcontplot 143–144
listplot 142
ln 25, 26
local 178–183
log 25, 26
log10 25
lowerbound 165–166

macro 27
map 58
map2 58
matrix 117
Matrix (command) 117–120, 141
Matrix (option) 119
MatrixInverse 127
max 49, 209
maxdigits 23
member 49, 52

min 49, 209, 210
minus 50
mod 203, 204
mul 61–62, 105, 170

next 155
Norm 126–127
normal 75, 197
not 46, 149
numelems 52
numer 77–78
numeric (option) 115–116
numeric (type) 62–63

od 150
odd 157
op 51–52, 78–79
option cache 196
option remember 195–196
or 46, 83, 149
Order 97, 115

parfrac 75
pdsolve 116
permute 65
PI 35–36
Pi 11, 21, 35–36
pi 35–36
piecewise 83
plot 133–138
plot3d 138
point (command) 66, 140–141
point (option) 138
pointline 138
pointplot 142, 144
points 142
polar (command) 29
polar (option) 29, 137
polarplot 138
polygon 138
polygonoutline 138
polynom 97
print 159–160, 162
printf 160–162
printlevel 158–159, 198
proc 174–197
procname 195
protect 36

quit 219
Re 28
read 220–221
red 136
restart 32–33, 39
return 175, 191–192
rhs 44–45, 114–115
RootOf 105, 108
row 118–119
rtablesize 122–123

save 221
scaling 137
Search 174
seq 58–62, 170
series (command) 97–99, 197
series (option) 115
set 63
showassumed 102
showstat 198–199
simplify 74–75
sin 25
sinh 25
solidcircle 141
solve 103–109
sort 174
spherical 145
sqrt 25, 74
style 138–139, 142
subs 79–80
subset 50
Sum 89, 91–92
sum 89–92
surd 30
surface 143–144
surfdata 143–144
symbol 141
symbolic 75
symbolsize 141

table 168, 172–173
tabular 172–173
tan 25
tanh 25
Telescoping 89–90
then 147–150
time 197

title 136
to 150–157
Transpose 127
trig 30
type 62–64, 171–173

unapply 84–86, 93, 114
unassign 32, 168
uneval 188
union 50
unprotect 36
unwith 65
upperbound 165–166
user 36

value 88, 89, 92, 94
vector 117
Vector (command) 117–120, 141, 164
Vector (option) 119
verboseproc 175, 198
view 134, 136–137

whattype 62, 63, 171
while 155–156
with 65
WRITE 221

Printed in the United States
by Baker & Taylor Publisher Services